Deterrence in an Era of Iranian Nuclear Proliferation

Deterrence in an Era of Iranian Nuclear Proliferation

Navid Hassibi

Lulu Press – Raleigh, NC

Library of Congress Control Number: 2012921016

ISBN 978-1-105-69869-9 (paperback)

ISBN 978-1-105-71251-7 (hardcover)

ISBN 978-1-105-71056-8 (eBook)

Portions of this book stem from the author's MA dissertation, titled: The Proliferation of Nuclear Weapons to Iran: Should the International Community be Worried? Submitted to the University of Manchester in 2008; available for viewing at the Joule Library/John Rylands University Library, Sackville Street Building, The University of Manchester.

Lulu Press, Inc., 3101 Hillsborough Street, Raleigh, NC 27607

Contents

Glossary

AEOI	Atomic Energy Organization of Iran
DIO	Defence Industries Organization
EU-3	France, the United Kingdom and Germany
GCC	Gulf Cooperation Council
IAEA	International Atomic Energy Agency
IRGC	Iranian Revolutionary Guards Corps
MAD	Mutually Assured Destruction
NCRI	National Council of Resistance of Iran
NPT	Treaty on the Non-proliferation of Nuclear Weapons
P5+1	France, the United Kingdom, Russia, China, the US and Germany
UAE	United Arab Emirates
UK	United Kingdom
UN	United Nations
US	United States
USSR	Union of Soviet Socialist Republics
WMD	Weapon(s) of mass destruction

Chapter One - Introduction

The Iranian nuclear program has been of grave concern to the international community, namely the West and Israel, since news broke in 2002 that Tehran clandestinely operated two nuclear facilities in Natanz and Arak. The Islamic Republic of Iran claims that it is exercising its inalienable right under Article IV of the Nuclear Non-Proliferation Treaty (NPT). The international community, namely the West and Israel, distrust Iran's motives and believe that Tehran is seeking to develop nuclear weapons.

Iran's clandestine nuclear development along with its rapid nuclear advancement and often bellicose negotiating strategy has triggered concern among the West and Israel. Their opposition to Iran's nuclear progress prompts the question as to whether their cause for concern is warranted. Would the Cold War concept of Mutually Assured Destruction (MAD) and hence nuclear deterrence not apply in a setting where the Islamic Republic of Iran possessed nuclear weapons? Proponents of nuclear deterrence believe that nuclear proliferation is not to be feared and that its efficiency has been proven during the Cold War between the United States and the Soviet Union. In this context, apprehension over Iranian nuclear proliferation is misplaced because deterrence would be in effect. Opponents of nuclear deterrence however claim that the Cold War was unique and that the two sides were on the brink of nuclear warfare on numerous occasions. Skeptics generally think that nuclear deterrence is flawed and as such, further nuclear proliferation ought to be avoided.

According to nuclear deterrence theory, there is no cause for concern with regards to the spread of nuclear weapons due to MAD; therefore in the Iranian context, deterrence ought to work. The international community should however be concerned due to the possibility of deterrence failures arising as a nuclear Iran may adopt a more aggressive and intimidating posture. Deterrence failures may occur due to internal deficiencies within the Islamic Republic. In addition, as it stands, it is difficult for the West and Israel to trust the regime in Tehran because of its poor track record consisting of domestic oppression and human rights violations; defiance of United Nations (UN) Security Council resolutions; suspected terrorism linkages; hostility toward Israel; an arms build-up; and an opaque nuclear program. It is critical to note at this juncture that according to the 2007 US National Intelligence Estimate, which represents the consensus of 16 American intelligence agencies, Iran halted its nuclear weapons program in 2003 but that the Iranian government is likely keeping its options open with respect to building a weapon.[1]

In order to reach a sound conclusion regarding whether the international community ought to be worried about Iran's nuclear proliferation, it would be prudent to explore the theories that explain why states seek to develop nuclear weapons. Identifying the motivational causes would help devise a solution that could potentially diffuse the situation. Nuclear deterrence theory will then be explored and analyzed as will the arguments against it. The theories will be used as a framework for ascertaining whether Iran's proliferation is worrisome. The Iranian nuclear program will then be discussed as will

---

[1] The New York Times, "U.S. Says Iran Ended Atomic Arms Work,"
http://www.nytimes.com/2007/12/03/world/middleeast/03cnd-iran.html

the motivating factors for Iran's nuclear pursuit. Theory will then be merged with practice as nuclear deterrence and its potential flaws are applied within an Iranian context. The results would then show a compelling argument as to why Iranian nuclear proliferation is or is not a cause for concern to the international community. Methods of nuclear proliferation prevention will also be examined as will their efficacy in an Iranian context. This will be done to describe the tools available to the international community when addressing Iran's suspected military nuclear ambitions. Finally, a policy option will be availed that reflects a pragmatic approach regarding the Iranian nuclear program.

Chapter Two - Why go nuclear?

Why is it that some countries choose to pursue a nuclear weapons program? To help answer this question, several theories of nuclear proliferation will be discussed and analyzed. These motivational causes of nuclear proliferation will be thoroughly inspected in this chapter.

Motivations for developing nuclear weapons

The first nuclear weapons were developed over sixty years ago for two primary reasons: first, to be instruments of compellence, that is to say, as a means to end the Second World War; and second, to serve as a projector of power.[2] Since then, nuclear proliferation has increased not only vertically, but also horizontally.[3] There have been thirteen nuclear weapons states since its inception in the early 1940s, however there are currently nine states in possession of nuclear weapons: seven declared nuclear powers – the United States, Russia, France, the United Kingdom, China, Pakistan, India, one ambiguous nuclear power – Israel, and North Korea, which allegedly conducted two underground nuclear tests, one in October 2006 and the other in May 2009. South Africa disassembled its stockpile in the early 1990s; Belarus, Kazakhstan, and the Ukraine transferred their stockpile to Russia a few years after the collapse of the Soviet Union. The gradual increase in the number of states with nuclear weapons begs the question why states

---

[2] Derek D. Smith, Deterring America (Cambridge: Cambridge University Press, 2006), p21.

[3] Vertical proliferation signifies the increase in stockpile of nuclear weapons while horizontal proliferation signifies the spread of nuclear weapons to more states.

seek to develop them. This section will discuss the theoretical perspectives on why nations choose to "go nuclear". The causes for nuclear proliferation can be categorized into the following three sets of hypotheses:

- Technological and bureaucratic imperative model
- International and domestic political model
- National security model

Technological and bureaucratic imperative model

The underlying reasoning of this particular model is that nuclear technology, in itself, is the impetus for states to go nuclear.[4] In other words, governments decide to "go nuclear" because the technology is available.[5] According to Bradley A. Thayer, technology causes proliferation and renders decision makers powerless to halt the obdurate lure of nuclear weapons.[6] Correspondingly, Stephen M. Meyer believes that once a nation acquires the capability to produce nuclear weaponry, it will inevitably do so due to a growing technological momentum.[7] Meyer, aware of the fact that not all technologically able states cross the nuclear threshold, claims that these states are keeping the option to develop nuclear weapons if need be.[8]

Similarly, some argue that the decision to proliferate is made by individuals within the scientific or defence bureaucracies of states,

---

[4] Stephen M. Meyer, The Dynamics of Nuclear Proliferation (Chicago: University of Chicago Press, 1984), p9.

[5] Ibid.

[6] Bradley A. Thayer, "The Causes of Nuclear Proliferation and the Utility of the Non-proliferation Regime," Security Studies (Spring 1995), vol 4, no 3: p18.

[7] Meyer, Dynamics, p9.

[8] Ibid, p5.

as they want to enhance the power of their respective bureaucracies.[9] Thayer aptly discusses the power that highly ranked bureaucrats possess in pursuing objectives that are related to their particular bureaucracy.[10] He claims that bureaucrats retain their own understanding and ideas about the obstacles the state faces and how they can best be resolved.[11]

International and domestic political model

The second category of hypotheses for seeking nuclear proliferation rests on a set of political variables with nuclear weapons being a policy option that can help a state pursue a foreign, and/or domestic objective.[12] According to this hypothesis, the inception of nuclear weapons programs can be better understood within the context of the following two groupings of motivations:

- International and regional political power and prestige
- Domestic political and economic motivations

International and regional political power and prestige

This grouping signifies that the possession of nuclear weapons can undoubtedly help a state "flex its muscles", giving it the ability to become an influential voice in international affairs by providing the capability to achieve foreign policy goals that were previously unattainable while being a conventional military power. As Gawdat Bahgat indicates, that the five nuclear powers acknowledged by the

---

[9] Priscilla Clapp and Morton Halperin, Bureaucratic Politics and Foreign Policy (Washington DC: Brookings Institution Press, 2007), p28, p39; see also Thayer, "The Causes of Nuclear Proliferation and the Utility of the Non-proliferation Regime," p15.

[10] Thayer, "Causes," p14.

[11] Ibid, p14.

[12] Meyer, Dynamics, p9.

NPT are also permanent members of the UN Security Council elucidates that nuclear weapons do in fact yield political influence.[13]

Similarly, a desire to possess international prestige, and maintain greatness is a deciding factor in developing nuclear weapons. For instance, prior to attaining their bomb, the British believed that failure to accept the challenge of atomic energy would have been interpreted as a retreat from greatness and an abandonment of power.[14] Relatedly, Charles de Gaulle believed that in order for France to be considered a great nation, it would have to develop nuclear weapons.[15]

The development of nuclear weapons by a particular state may encourage the proliferation of similar weapons by rival states seeking to improve their international and regional status. According to Kenneth N. Waltz, nuclear states may come in pairs, as the proliferation of one state is likely to motivate a rival to follow suit.[16] An obvious example of this is the Soviet Union's development of nuclear weapons as a direct response to the American nuclear hegemony which existed in the mid to late 1940s.

Domestic political and economic motivations

The second grouping is associated with the perception that nuclear proliferation derives from domestic political and economic conditions, meaning that a state may decide to pursue nuclear weapons as a means

---

[13] Gawdat Bahgat, "Nuclear Proliferation: The Islamic Republic of Iran," International Studies Perspective (2006), no 7: p126.

[14] Thayer, "Causes," p8.

[15] Ibid, p7.

[16] Scott D. Sagan and Kenneth N. Waltz, The Spread of Nuclear Weapons (New York: W.W. Norton & Company, 2003), p12; see also Bahgat, "Nuclear Proliferation: The Islamic Republic of Iran," p125.

of diverting attention away from domestic turmoil.[17] Meyer articulates that this is a technological approach to "rallying round the flag".[18]

Another possible motive for developing nuclear weapons might be the burden on the economy of a particular state as a result of maintaining and developing conventional military forces.[19] In other words, nuclear weapons can be more cost effective.[20] One can therefore argue that the option to pursue nuclear weapons is taken with the aim of getting more "bang for the buck".[21]

National security model

The third category of hypotheses for pursuing nuclear weapons is driven by military and security incentives. It suggests that states seek nuclear weapons for either tactical usage or deterrence when confronted with a military threat from abroad.[22] This causal factor seems to be the primary reason why states pursue nuclear weapons. For example, the Soviet Union developed its nuclear capability in response to the American bomb and the threat of US global hegemony. The People's Republic of China developed its arsenal because of fears of Soviet and US aggression. The Indian nuclear weapons program was developed as a consequence of China's proliferation. In riposte, the Pakistanis proliferated as well. The French developed their bomb because of general suspicions toward American security guarantees and out of fear for the Soviets.[23] The Soviets were also on the mind of the British

---

[17] Meyer, Dynamics, p63.

[18] Ibid.

[19] Ibid, p65.

[20] Sagan and Waltz, Spread, p153.

[21] Meyer, Dynamics, p65.

[22] Ibid, p47.

when they made the decision to "go nuclear". Israel acquired its ambiguous "nukes" in response to continuous hostilities by its Middle Eastern neighbours, in addition to its desire to be militarily superior to them.[24] Most analysts agree that perceived threats to national security provide the fundamental motive for governments to attain nuclear weapons.[25] Along similar lines, some argue that the awesome might of the American military provides reasons for states to acquire these weapons of mass destruction (WMDs).[26] As Waltz puts it, the US' conventional dominance spurs other countries to resort to unconventional means.[27]

Summary

The motivations behind the pursuit of nuclear weapons have been discussed in this chapter. It is quite evident that nuclear proliferation cannot be explained by a single causal factor. The possible reasons for which states decide to proliferate are contingent on many variables. These causal mechanisms can emanate either from within the state or externally.

It has been discussed that technical and bureaucratic imperatives may lead some states to develop a nuclear capability, or a nuclear option. Domestic conditions such as civil unrest may lead a particular government to think of a way to divert the public's attention away from the turmoil at home and onto an apparatus, such as nuclear weapons, that may ignite nationalistic sentiments. Economic benefits

---

[23] Thayer, "Causes," p28.

[24] Ibid, p30.

[25] Bahgat, "Islamic," p125.

[26] Ibid, p126.

[27] Sagan and Waltz, Spread, p150.

have also been mentioned as a causal factor to proliferate as has the enmity between rivals. States may also desire to embark on a quest to attain nuclear weapons as a means to gain international and regional prestige and power. It may also do so in accordance with the national security model, that is to say, to achieve military and security incentives. It has been argued that this model is the major cause of nuclear proliferation. According to one academic, only by acquiring a nuclear capability can states gain security from nuclear coercion and major wars.[28] The primary instrument of the national security model is nuclear deterrence and as such, it will be further examined in the following section.

---

[28] Thayer, "Causes," p35.

Chapter Three - Theoretical approaches to nuclear deterrence

The first part of this chapter will deal with nuclear deterrence theory and its supporting arguments. As a prevalent proponent of nuclear deterrence, the work of Kenneth N. Waltz will be predominantly used to better understand the arguments of this perspective. The second part consists of opposing views to nuclear deterrence theory, followed by a comprehensive discussion about methods of nuclear proliferation prevention. The aim of this chapter is to provide a theoretical framework in order to better understand the proliferation of nuclear weapons and the effects of nuclear deterrence.

Nuclear deterrence theory

That the spread of nuclear weapons would bring forth more stability in the international system seems initially oxymoronic, yet the logic behind this line of thinking rests on what has been coined in the early days of the Cold War as Mutually Assured Destruction (MAD). The idea behind MAD is that if two or more states possess nuclear weapons, neither side will initiate a first strike because of the other's second strike capability. The ability to retaliate with a second strike thus becomes a deterrent force which would inhibit the aggressor from taking initial action. Alternatively, deterrence can be interpreted as a means of persuading an adversary that the costs of a particular action will outweigh any potential benefit.[29] Supporters of deterrence theory and its efficacy believe that the apprehension over the proliferation of

---

[29] Smith, Deterring, p17.

nuclear weapons is erroneous and that there should not be a cause for concern.

Proponents of nuclear deterrence theory

Kenneth N. Waltz, one of the more prominent proponents of nuclear deterrence, believes that not only will deterrence work - as it has in the past during the Cold War between the United States and the Soviet Union and between the Soviet Union and the People's Republic of China – but that the spread of nuclear weapons may be conducive to international security.[30] Waltz has reached this unusual conclusion due to his strong conviction in deterrence theory and its ability to:

- Dissuade possible attack from an aggressor thus increasing a state's security
- Reduce the likelihood of nuclear war
- Increase regional stability
- Decrease the prospect of arms races

Nuclear deterrence and the dissuasion of possible attack

As a notable structural realist or neo-realist, it comes as no surprise that Waltz's prognosis of the nuclear issue rests on the belief that states coexist in a condition of anarchy and that self-help is the basis of such an anarchic order.[31] This also means that the most important manner in which states can help themselves is by providing for their own security which is one of the primary reasons states make the decision to pursue nuclear weapons.[32] Waltz explains that nuclear forces are not defensive

---

[30] John Simpson and Anthony G. McGrew, <u>The International Nuclear Non-proliferation System: Challenges and Choices</u> (London: Macmillan Press, 1984), p77.

[31] Sagan and Waltz, <u>Spread</u>, p5.

by nature and that they are meant to be an offensive weapon with only one purpose, to inflict punishment. This ability to punish thus becomes the deterrent.[33]   As a result, dissuasion by deterrence functions by terrifying a state out of attacking due to the possible catastrophic scope of a retaliatory response.[34]

Nuclear deterrence and the likelihood of nuclear war

Those who oppose Waltz's view that the spread of nuclear weapons should be embraced with open arms argue that the risks of nuclear warfare increase with horizontal proliferation. Waltz refutes this claim by stating that the presence of nuclear weapons makes war less likely and points to the fact that nuclear weapons have not been fired in a world in which more than one country has had them.[35]

Waltz further reasons that:

- states are not likely to run major risks for minor gains;
- and states act with less care if the expected costs of war are low and with more care if they are high.[36]

In other words, the proliferation of nuclear weapons would not induce nuclear warfare because as Waltz puts it:

> "If countries armed with nuclear weapons go to war with each other, they do so knowing that their suffering may be unlimited. In a conventional world, one is uncertain about

---

[32] Ibid.

[33] Ibid.

[34] Ibid.

[35] Ibid, p33.

[36] Ibid, p6-7.

winning or losing. In a nuclear world, one is uncertain about surviving or being annihilated."[37]

Put differently, nuclear weapons produce what Joseph Nye calls the "crystal ball" effect. With conventional weapons, the crystal ball and hence the outcome is clouded but with nuclear weapons, the outcome is perfectly clear.[38]

Nuclear deterrence and regional stability

A concern among opponents of nuclear proliferation is the regional impact of such a device and whether stability can be maintained after nuclear weapons have been developed. According to Waltz, new nuclear states may come in pairs and may even share a border between them.[39] If these states are bitter enemies, one may believe that they will be unable to resist the usage of such horrific devices.[40] Waltz discards this belief by citing the hostilities between the United States, the Soviet Union and the People's Republic of China during the Cold War. He states that nuclear weapons caused them to deal cautiously with one another while even pointing to the fact that the Soviets and the Chinese shared a long border.[41] Waltz explains this behaviour by claiming that linkages are infrequently present between bitterness and a state's willingness to run high risks.[42] Regional stability is enhanced under deterrence theory because it induces caution amongst the constituents.

---

[37] Ibid, p9.

[38] Albert Carnesale, Paul Doty, Stanley Hoffman, Samuel P. Huntington, Joseph S. Nye Jr. and Scott Sagan, Living with Nuclear Weapons (Cambridge: Harvard University Press, 1983), p44.

[39] Sagan and Waltz, Spread, p12.

[40] Ibid.

[41] Ibid.

[42] Ibid.

The reoccurring theme of nuclear deterrence is Mutually Assured Destruction, and as such, nuclear proliferation should not be feared in a regional setting. After all, a country that launches a first strike has to fear a retributive blow.

Opponents of deterrence theory fear that governments that are radical domestically will behave in a similar fashion regionally by using their nuclear weapons to pursue revolutionary objectives.[43] Waltz subdues this fear by stating that few nations have been radical in their conduct of foreign policy.[44] Radical regimes want to stay in power therefore they would not risk losses of any proportion according to Waltz.[45]

Nuclear deterrence and arms races

For some, it is logical to assume that nuclear proliferants may engage in arms build-ups or arms races, as was the case during the Cold War, but as Waltz articulates, this concern is exaggerated. He believes that the spread of nuclear weapons is likely to decrease military spending by proliferants.[46] He reasons that force comparisons are irrelevant in a nuclear world and as a result, strategic arms races are rendered pointless.[47] The underlying argument is that nuclear deterrence eliminates incentives for conventional arms build-ups.[48] Large conventional forces neither add to nor detract from a state's first or second strike capability.[49]

---

[43] Ibid.

[44] Ibid.

[45] Ibid, p14.

[46] Ibid, p29.

[47] Ibid, p30.

[48] Ibid, p31.

Summary

In brief, nuclear deterrence theory relies on a state's ability to discourage attack from an aggressor by threatening retaliatory punishment thereby assuring Mutually Assured Destruction. Some believe that the spread of nuclear weapons ought not to be feared but rather embraced because of its stabilizing features. In this context, nuclear deterrence is believed not only to discourage attack thus increasing a country's security, but to also reduce the frequency and intensity of war; to increase regional stability; and to decrease arms races between nations. Proponents of deterrence theory claim that its reliability has been proven during the Cold War.

As Waltz puts it:

> "Nuclear weapons reduced the chances of war between the United States and the Soviet Union and between the Soviet Union and China. One must expect them to have similar effects elsewhere. Where nuclear weapons threaten to make the cost of wars immense, who will dare to start them?"[50]

Skeptics of nuclear deterrence theory

Opponents of horizontal nuclear diffusion believe that the role of nuclear deterrence as a guarantor of stability between nuclear proliferants is misplaced.

As Scott D. Sagan exclaims:

> "The United States and the Soviet Union survived the Cold War and did not use their nuclear weapons. This should be

---

[49] Ibid, p32.

[50] Sagan and Waltz, Spread, p44.

cause for celebration and not be an excuse for inaction with either arms control or non-proliferation. The fact that two states performed this feat one time should not lead us to think that other states can safely do it again."[51]

Those who do not welcome nuclear proliferation and reject nuclear deterrence theory fear that nuclear deterrence is flawed and that the spread of nuclear weapons will be detrimental to the international system because:

- The risk of nuclear warfare will increase
- Regional stability will decrease
- Terrorists may acquire nuclear weapons
- Deficiencies among new nuclear states will increase accidental and/or deliberate usage of nuclear weapons

Nuclear deterrence and the likelihood of nuclear war

Kenneth N. Waltz argues that the causes of war are purged with the introduction of nuclear deterrence. This line of thinking may be warranted if the proliferators are seeking self-security and are hence, defensively motivated, as Waltz suggests they are.[52] If however, one of the proliferators is offensively motivated or simply undertakes an action that can be wrongfully interpreted as invasive then the chances of war increase.[53] The Cuban missile crisis of 1962 exemplifies this argument. The Soviet warheads that were deployed in Cuba, although declared to be merely of a defensive nature, were seen as offensive by

---

[51] Ibid, p87.

[52] Thayer, "Causes," p47.

[53] Ibid.

the Americans. Consequently, the superpowers were led to what many believe was the brink of nuclear warfare.

Waltz's argument can further be refuted by using a quantitative lens. It can be argued that in a world which sees more states possessing nuclear weapons, utilization of such weapons are likely to increase.[54] As former US Secretary of Defense Robert McNamara once said, a world with a dozen or more nuclear powers would be a dangerous one.[55] This anxiety over nuclear proliferation rests on the belief that the more fingers there are on the trigger, the higher the prospects of that trigger being pulled.[56] Contrary to the ostensibly pacifying effect of American and Soviet nuclear weapons during the Cold War, one academic notes that their wider spread is commonly considered to be dangerous.[57] Joseph Nye has written that under many conditions, the proliferation of even a single bomb in some non-nuclear states may be more susceptible to usage than the addition of a thousand more warheads to the American and Soviet stockpiles.[58] This line of thinking suggests that new proliferants may not be as "mature" as the established nuclear weapons states and might consequently resort to the usage of a nuclear device.

Another contending view as to why the risks of nuclear warfare increase with more proliferation rests on the idea that an accidental war might erupt if the leader of a new nuclear state delegates the authority

---

[54] Devin T. Hagerty, The Consequences of Nuclear Proliferation: Lessons from South Asia (Cambridge: MIT Press, 1998), p16.

[55] Bader, Weapons, p106; see also Waltz and Sagan, Spread, p11.

[56] Hans Blix, "Foreword," in Joseph F. Pilat and Robert E Pendley, eds., Beyond 1995: The Future of the NPT Regime (New York: Plenum Press, 1990), p.ix.

[57] Hagerty, Consequences, p11.

[58] Joseph S. Nye Jr., "NPT: The Logic of Inequality," Foreign Policy (Summer 1985), no 59: p128.

to use nuclear weapons to lower level commanders.[59] An accidental launch of a nuclear weapon might occur if the lower level commander misinterprets a threat. Presently, commanding officers of British Trident nuclear submarines have the discretion to use nuclear weapons in the event of contact failure with headquarters. Although the British are unlikely to accidentally launch nuclear weapons, this example reveals that the delegation of authority does exist and could be hazardous if it were to happen in a "rogue" state or a developing country that is inexperienced or immature in a nuclear sense.

An additional flaw of nuclear deterrence theory for the skeptics is that it assumes that states are rational actors and that as a result will act reasonably by not jeopardizing and provoking its own destruction.[60] History shows however that every now and then, states are willing to accept enormous risks, even ones that compromise their own existence, for what they perceive to be important causes.[61]

It is important to note that as previously stated, nuclear weapons have not been used in a time where two or more states possessed them. Nevertheless they have been used twice, which confirms their status as instruments of war, not devices of peace. In addition, the presence of low yield tactical nuclear weapons makes it a reality that offensive nuclear weapons do in fact exist. This makes it a possibility that a new nuclear state might convert its strategic deterrent into a tactical weapon designed for offensive purposes consequently impeding the effects of nuclear deterrence.

---

[59] Sagan and Waltz, Spread, p80.

[60] Smith, Deterring, p26.

[61] Ibid.

Nuclear deterrence and regional stability

Waltz's argument that nuclear deterrence can increase regional stability is problematic to skeptics. Stephen M. Meyer examines the effects of nuclear proliferation on a regional level and concludes that even if a new nuclear weapons state does not have a rival in the region, its action may nevertheless stimulate further proliferation.[62] Meyer grounds his examination on three premises:

1) though a neighbour may not be presently a rival, it could be one in the future;
2) an inclination to keep up with one's neighbours is crafted by each new nuclear proliferant;
3) and the emergence of a new nuclear weapons power will induce other states to reconsider their own positions in light of one more state's decision to go nuclear.[63]

In addition to the above, the proliferation of nuclear weapons to a conflict prone region would destabilize an already volatile area. There is no guarantee that a state will not utilize a nuclear device on another. One scholar notes that nuclear deterrence is at root a psychological phenomenon and as a result it will never be possible to be certain of another person's state of mind.[64]

The close proximity between adversaries in a regional setting is not conducive to stability. It allows for less time to react and fewer margins for error in the event that a threat was perceived.[65] The likelihood of false alarms would be greater in new nuclear proliferation

---

[62] Meyer, Dynamics, p64.

[63] Ibid.

[64] Smith, Deterring, p16.

[65] Sagan and Waltz, Spread, p79; see also Hagerty, Consequences, p13.

regions and the ability to distinguish between a real threat and a misperceived one would be reduced due to time constraints thus decreasing regional stability.

Nuclear weapons and terrorism

The events of September 11th 2001 have put terrorism on the forefront of international security. As a result, the distress over linkages between the spread of nuclear weapons and terrorism has grown. The primary concern is that horizontal nuclear proliferation may increase the chances of WMDs finding their way into the hands of terrorists. In this context, a nuclear device developed by a "rogue" state or a developing country may be transferred to a terrorist group, either by consent or as a result of espionage.

It can be argued that nuclear deterrence against a non-state actor such as a terrorist organization is futile. Nuclear deterrence and hence, the ability to threaten punishment, is difficult when the adversary believes that their cause is worth killing and dying for.[66] The recipient of a terrorist nuclear strike would not be able to retaliate accordingly with the notion of MAD because the aggressor is obscure, therefore rendering nuclear deterrence ineffective. The alternative would be to retaliate with a nuclear or conventional second strike against the country that sponsors and/or harbours that particular terrorist group. Regardless of what the victim state does, nuclear deterrence is proven to be unsuccessful in this setting because the occurrence of a first strike could not be prevented.

---

[66] Sagan and Waltz, Spread, p161.

Nuclear proliferation and deficiencies within new nuclear states

There is reason to believe that the proliferation of nuclear weapons will increase among states with deficiencies which can be categorically divided into the following:

- Technical deficiencies
- Organizational deficiencies
- Political deficiencies (international and domestic)

Nuclear proliferation and technical deficiencies

Those who doubt the efficiency of nuclear deterrence argue that new proliferators will be incapable to handle and maintain their nuclear weapons and as a consequence, the probability of accidents occurring will increase.

Waltz refutes this concern and claims that all nuclear states have lived through a time when their forces were crude and that they were all able to overcome it.[67] He adds that new proliferators may indeed be technically deficient but that if they have successfully crossed the nuclear threshold then they possess the adequate technical expertise to maintain them.[68] According to Waltz, the technically deficient proliferants will have every incentive to take good care of their nuclear capabilities because they will not want to risk retaliation due to an accident.[69]

The skeptics disclaim Waltz's line of thinking by referring to the number of incidents the US has had with its own nuclear weapons. One example shows that even the US' safety record with regards to

---

[67] Ibid, p21.

[68] Ibid.

[69] Ibid.

nuclear weapons is imperfect. In 2007, a B-52 bomber transported missiles, whose nuclear warheads were supposed to be removed, across the continental United States.[70] The warheads were accidentally left on the missiles thus breaching security regulations surrounding nuclear weapons.[71] The warheads were not armed, reducing the chances of a nuclear detonation, but had the bomber encountered difficulties while in flight and crashed, radioactive fallout would have spread all across the region.

Opaque proliferation may also cause technical deficiencies for new nuclear proliferators due to the clandestine nature of the program which prohibits external monitoring that could potentially increase overall safety.[72] Also, as Sagan points out, the inability to have full scale nuclear weapons tests hinders the progress of operative safety designs.[73]

Technical shortcomings ought to be feared due to the possible risk increase of unforeseen accidents. Such deficiencies can lead to catastrophic incidents at processing plants and may even lead to nuclear meltdowns which would create hazardous nuclear fallout. The incidents at Three Mile Island and Chernobyl are evidence that nuclear accidents do occur, even in fully industrialized nations.[74] If such occurrences can happen in highly developed countries then who is to say that it could not happen again in a technically deficient one?

---

[70] CNN, "Air Force Investigates Mistaken Transport of Nuclear Warheads," (http://edition.cnn.com/2007/US/09/05/loose.nukes/index.html)

[71] Ibid.

[72] Sagan and Waltz, Spread, p78-79.

[73] Ibid; see also Hagerty, Consequences, p40.

[74] Hagerty, Consequences, p30.

Nuclear proliferation and organizational deficiencies

According to Sagan, nuclear deterrence is defective because of what he labels as the organization perspective theory. The central tenet of this theorem is that professional military organizations – due to common biases, rigid routines and insular interests – exhibit organizational behaviours that are likely to lead to deterrence failures.[75] He argues that military establishments, unless managed through checks and balances, and under the control of strong civilian authorities, are unlikely to fulfill the functional prerequisites for nuclear deterrence.[76]

Sagan supports his claims by reasoning that large organizations function with limited rationality, meaning that they use simple mechanisms to comprehend and react to ambiguity with regards to external relations.[77] For instance, organizations develop routines and procedures to govern behaviour as opposed to reasoning and rationality.[78] Moreover, members of the organization have biases stemming from past experiences, training and current obligations.[79] In addition, these organizations usually possess conflicting goals and the manner in which they are pursued is very much political.[80] As a result, the interests of the few in that specific organization are served. Sagan believes that organizational perspective theory applies best to the military. Discernible examples of this approach can be seen when examining country's which fall victim to a military *coup d'etat*.

---

[75] Sagan and Waltz, Spread, p47; see also Smith, Deterring, p32.

[76] Sagan and Waltz, Spread, p47.

[77] Ibid, p51.

[78] Ibid.

[79] Ibid.

[80] Ibid, p52.

Nuclear proliferation and political deficiencies

Political inadequacies in a new nuclear state can very much affect the stability of nuclear deterrence. These deficiencies can stem either domestically or externally. A government that is oppressive may have higher chances of encountering revolt thus increasing civil unrest and domestic instability. Waltz claims that domestic uncertainty is not problematic to the effects of nuclear deterrence, while Sagan refutes this claim by stating that domestic instability can produce accidental detonations.[81]

Another reason to fear the failure of nuclear deterrence rests on the prospect of unpredictable leaders with unknown levels of risk tolerance.[82] As Kathleen C. Bailey notes, ruthlessness and lack of sanity has led governments to use chemical weapons on its own citizenry thus giving credence to the argument that some leaders may be irresponsible with such devastating weapons.[83] Similarly, Derek D. Smith explains that deterrence is at root a psychological concept therefore feelings of pride and defiance can amalgamate into a determination to use nuclear weapons.[84] Time pressure, fatigue and anxiety can have detrimental effects on the psyche of an unpredictable leader which can result in desperation and panic which is unquestionably damaging to the prospects of nuclear deterrence at a time of crisis.[85]

---

[81] Ibid, p82.

[82] Smith, Deterring, p29; see also Tom Sauer, Nuclear Arms Control: Nuclear Deterrence in the Post Cold War Period (London: Macmillan Press, 1998), p5.

[83] Kathleen C. Bailey, Doomsday Weapons in the Hands of Many: The Arms Control Challenge of the 1990s (Urbana: University of Illinois Press, 1991), p2.

[84] Smith, Deterring, p30.

[85] Ibid, p32; see also Sauer, Arms, p4.

A radical fundamentalist government may also seek to expand its fanatical ideologies and can benefit from nuclear weapons.[86] Such a state may seek to destroy a rival for what it may perceive to be as serving a higher end.[87] In this context, a radical state may initiate a first strike with the hope of receiving a devastating second strike from a rival, justifying them as acts of martyrdom.[88]

Opaque proliferation, which was briefly mentioned earlier, adds to the political deficiency of a state. Opaque proliferation is the surreptitious development of nuclear weapons coupled with public deniability and an undisputed support for global non-proliferation.[89] Opacity confirms a state's lack of responsibility due to the absence of adherence to global norms. States which proliferate in this manner usually do so in violation of international law.[90] The mere nature of opacity suggests that states that acquire nuclear weapons in this fashion are untrustworthy and are more susceptible to using them.

Summary

This section has dealt with the opposing views regarding nuclear deterrence theory. In brief, the skeptics argue that with an inclination in nuclear proliferation: the risks of nuclear war increase; regional stability decreases; terrorist access to nuclear materials increase; technical, organizational, and/or political deficiencies existing within new proliferants may lead to accidental or deliberate usage of nuclear weapons. For these reasons, skeptics of nuclear deterrence believe that

---

[86] Sauer, Arms, p4.

[87] Smith, Deterring, p38.

[88] Ibid, p39.

[89] Hagerty, Consequences, p40.

[90] Ibid.

the spread of nuclear weapons will increase instability and as such, nuclear proliferation ought to be feared and prevented.

Conclusion

Nuclear deterrence theory dictates that a state in possession of nuclear weapons has the ability to persuade an adversary that a first strike against it would be foolish due to the punishing second strike blow that may be reciprocated. Furthermore, it was discussed that nuclear deterrence is beneficial to global stability because of its ability to: increase a state's security; reduce the likelihood of war; increase regional stability; and decrease arms build-ups. Proponents of nuclear deterrence refer to the fact that it has been proven to work during the Cold War.

Conversely, the skeptics of nuclear deterrence believe that more nuclear weapons would be detrimental to the stability of the international system because it would increase the likelihood of nuclear war; decrease regional stability; aid terrorists in their quest to attain WMDs; and lead to accidental or deliberate usage due to technical, organizational and political deficiencies within new nuclear states.

The effects of nuclear deterrence are not a matter of physical laws and hence do not have to be consistent from case to case. The fact that nuclear weapons have not been used in a world where more than one state possessed them seems to suggest that rationality within the actors has prevailed thus far. However, as Joseph Nye says:

"There can be no decisive answer in the debate over the effects of proliferation. Particular outcomes may differ. Some cases may start a disastrous chain of events; other cases may turn out to have benign effects."[91]

The theoretical approaches to nuclear proliferation discussed in chapters 2 and 3 will provide the necessary skeletal perspectives needed in order to accurately examine the proliferation of nuclear weapons to Iran and whether it is a cause for concern for the international community.

---

[91] Joseph S. Nye Jr., "Maintaining a Non-proliferation Regime," International Organization (Winter 1981), vol 35, no 1: p33.

Chapter Four - Nuclear proliferation prevention

For those advocating a halt to nuclear proliferation, preventive measures may be a solution to decreasing the spread of nuclear weapons. Such preventive measures would have the aim of persuading and/or coercing a state into discontinuing its nuclear weapons program either willingly or unwillingly.[92] Preventive measures can be categorized into the following:

- Prevention through domestic changes
- Prevention through diplomacy
- Prevention through non-proliferation regimes
- Prevention through the use of force

Prevention through domestic changes

A change in the domestic political landscape may trigger a reversal in the decision to pursue nuclear weapons. It can be argued that states can reverse their nuclear policies after their government undergoes a transformation from military to civilian and hence democratic rule.[93]

A change in attitude of the ruling elite may also be a tipping point in a state's quest to pursue nuclear proliferation. In this *milieu*, the leader(s) of a particular country may discontinue the state's nuclear program in good faith hoping that its actions may clean its slate – resulting in the reintegration of that state into the international community. Libya's nuclear rollback in 2003 due to Colonel Qaddafi's

---

[92] Smith, Deterring, p95.

[93] Bahgat, "Islamic," p127.

desire to take his country back into the international fold is an example of a domestic change that can prevent nuclear proliferation.[94]

Prevention through diplomacy

Preventing a country from acquiring nuclear weapons by diplomatic means consists of a strategy that revolves around dialogue and negotiations between those seeking prevention and the proliferator. The objective of the dialogue is to dissuade the nuclear proliferator from either crossing the nuclear threshold; or to persuade it to disband and dismantle its nuclear weapons. In order to successfully use diplomacy as a tool of non-proliferation, a balance of carrots and sticks may have to be used. Finding the perfect equilibrium of incentives and disincentives may lead to a successful abandonment of the proliferator's nuclear ambition. The offered incentives would need to address the proliferator's concerns and reasons for wanting to "go nuclear". Disincentives would be applied when the country seeking nuclear weapons acts uncooperatively or when it goes against agreements it has assented to. Disincentives can take the form of bilateral or multilateral sanctions and embargoes. An example demonstrating successful diplomatic non-proliferation strategy is Ukraine's removal of former Soviet warheads from its territory in 1996.[95] The collapse of the Soviet Union left a large stockpile of nuclear weapons in the Ukraine, which was reluctant in transferring the warheads to Russia. With a series of negotiations however, the Ukraine agreed to remove all nuclear weaponry from its territory in addition to

---

[94] BBC, "Libya's Secret WMD,"
(http://news.bbc.co.uk/1/hi/world/middle_east/3336109.stm)

[95] Federation of American Scientists, "Nuclear Weapons in the Former Soviet Union,"
(http://www.fas.org/spp/starwars/crs/91-144.htm)

signing the NPT in exchange for US and international foreign aid; nuclear reactor fuel rods; fiscal compensation for the removal of the weapons; and informal mutual tripartite security guarantees between the US, Russia and itself.[96]

Prevention through non-proliferation regimes

The goal of the nuclear non-proliferation system is to discourage the spread of nuclear weapons through the usage of rules, protocols, norms, procedures and institutions that regulate the diffusion of nuclear technology.[97] These agreements exist chiefly to ensure that nuclear technology is attained and employed explicitly for peaceful purposes while minimizing the incentives of nuclear weapons proliferation.[98] The major regimes of non-proliferation consist of the International Atomic Energy Agency (IAEA), and the Nuclear Non-proliferation Treaty (NPT).

The International Atomic Energy Agency (IAEA)

Established in 1957, the IAEA and its safeguards are considered to be a major defence against nuclear proliferation.[99] The organization was created in order to apply a uniform set of safeguards to nuclear undertakings so that only peaceful benefits would be gained.[100]

The mechanisms that the IAEA has at its disposal consist of a combination of on-site inspections, audits of nuclear material –

---

[96] Ibid.

[97] Simpson and McGrew, International, p4; see also Sauer, Arms, p36.

[98] Simpson and McGrew, International, p4.

[99] Ibid, p39.

[100] Mitchell Reiss, Without the Bomb: The Politics of Nuclear Non-proliferation (New York: Columbia University Press, 1988), p14.

accounting and inventory procedures – and a variety of surveillance techniques.[101] It is important to note that the IAEA safeguards were not designed to be barriers against proliferation but rather to serve as a deterrent to a state from diverting safeguarded nuclear material to a clandestine nuclear weapons program.[102] If a state is caught diverting safeguarded material to a weapons program it does so knowing that the IAEA will detect the diversion, and in turn, report the matter to the UN Security Council which may act to impose sanctions.[103]

Critics of the IAEA system argue that while the safeguards apply to signatories of the NPT, they do not apply to non-members of the treaty which means that the IAEA cannot verify whether there is weapons diversion in a particular non-member state.[104]

The Nuclear Non-Proliferation Treaty (NPT)

The NPT was initiated in 1968 and was in effect by 1970.[105] With over one hundred eighty members, it is widely regarded as the cornerstone of the non-proliferation regime. There are only four states that are not currently members of the treaty: Israel, India, and Pakistan which never signed on; and North Korea which withdrew in 2003.[106]

The primary objectives of the NPT are enclosed within the first several provisions of the treaty. Article I prohibits the nuclear weapons

---

[101] Ibid.

[102] Simpson and McGrew, International, p39; Reiss, Without, p14.

[103] Simpson and McGrew, International, p39.

[104] Ibid.

[105] Reiss, Without, p19; see also UN, "Treaty on the Non-proliferation of Nuclear Weapons," (http://www.un.org/Depts/dda/WMD/treaty/)

[106] American Society of International Law, "North Korea's Withdrawal from the NPT," (http://www.asil.org/insights/insigh96.htm)

states from transferring nuclear weapons to any other country.[107] Article II imposes an obligation on the non-nuclear states not to develop nuclear weapons.[108] Article III states that non-nuclear members of the treaty are required to conclude a safeguards agreement with the IAEA which would allow that organization to carry out its purpose.[109] Article IV guarantees the inalienable right of all members of the treaty to develop peaceful nuclear energy through transfers of equipment, materials, scientific and technological information with other countries.[110]

The NPT regime has received a great deal of criticism primarily due to the fact that non-members do not need to adhere to its provisions. Pakistan and India, non-signatories of the treaty developed nuclear weapons which exemplifies a weakness of the NPT. Furthermore, many observers claim that there are loopholes within the treaty that aid nuclear proliferation.[111] The NPT allows the transfer of nuclear materials and technology between members. The dual use materials and technology can easily be clandestinely diverted to a weapons program. Many argue that North Korea's nuclear program developed in such a manner.[112]

---

[107] US State Department, "Non-Proliferation Treaty,"
(http://www.state.gov/www/global/arms/treaties/npt1.html)

[108] Ibid.

[109] Ibid.

[110] Ibid; see also Reiss, Without, p20.

[111] BBC, "Pros and Cons of the NPT,"
(http://news.bbc.co.uk/1/hi/world/americas/4491003.stm)

[112] Ibid.

Prevention through the use of force

If negotiations to rollback or to dismantle a state's nuclear weapons program fail, members of the international community might take it upon themselves to act forcefully in order to prevent the proliferation of nuclear weapons to that particular state. A preventive or preemptive strike might be the policy option chosen to deny a state what it perceives as being its prerogative to develop nuclear weapons.[113]

Preventive strikes

A preventive strike is a state's forceful response to a long term threat.[114] It is based on the concept that it is better to fight now while the costs are low rather than later when the costs are high.[115] A preventive strike against a nuclear installation was first undertaken in 1981 when the Israelis destroyed the Iraqi nuclear complex at Osirak and again in 2007 when the Israelis struck an alleged nuclear facility inside Syria.[116] According to Waltz, the Israelis struck the Iraqi plants at the right moment because the Iraqi nuclear program was still in an embryonic stage guaranteeing that the development of nuclear weapons had not yet occurred.[117] Waltz argues however that the victim of a preventive strike, in this case Iraq, will in all likelihood resume its nuclear program, which Iraq did, therefore the state seeking prevention has to either be prepared to repeat the strikes for as long as it takes, or to occupy and control the country.[118] In this setting, a preventive military strike may only serve as a short term solution.

---

[113] Smith, Deterring, p117-118.

[114] Ibid.

[115] Ibid.

[116] Sagan and Waltz, Spread, p18.

[117] Ibid.

Preemptive strikes

A preemptive attack is based on evidence that an enemy threat is imminent. In this context, a state about to cross the nuclear threshold may be attacked by a state seeking to deny it nuclear weapons.[119] Forceful preemptive measures may be difficult because a state would be in an advanced stage of nuclear development with capabilities that are unknown to the outside.[120] As Waltz exclaims, a rudimentary nuclear capability is enough to make one's own severe punishment a reality.[121] The belief that North Korea's nuclear program was highly sophisticated prevented the international community from taking military action against it which validates the claim that preemptive military measures are not an effective tool in combating nuclear proliferation.[122]

Summary

The analysis of nuclear proliferation prevention methods revealed that the inhibition of the spread of nuclear weapons can be accomplished through domestic changes; bilateral and multilateral diplomacy; through the usage of non-proliferation regimes such as the IAEA and the NPT, and through the use of preventive or preemptive force. Each method possesses imperfections, especially the latter method which could at best serve only as a short term solution.

---

[118] Ibid, p19.

[119] Smith, Deterring, p116.

[120] Sagan and Waltz, Spread, p18.

[121] Ibid, p19.

[122] Bahgat, "Islamic," p129; see also Ray Takeyh, "Iran Builds the Bomb," Survival (Winter 2004-2005), vol 46, no 4: p54.

Chapter Five - The Iranian nuclear program

The first section consists of a brief chronological timeline of the Iranian nuclear program. Iran's nuclear ambitions will be explored in the following section using the motivating causes described in chapter two. The third section will consist of a discussion of possible Iranian postures should they acquire nuclear weapons.

Setting the scene

The Iranians argue that they are developing peaceful nuclear energy, under the auspices of Article IV of the NPT, to generate electricity. They also claim that they are dedicated to mastering the fuel cycle in order to become a future supplier of nuclear fuel.[123] Tehran justifies its interest in nuclear technology by referring to its need to diversify its energy sources which are feeling the strains of a rapidly growing population and an increase in domestic oil consumption.[124] Iran's ambitions are problematic for the West and Israel. By desiring to possess the fuel cycle, the Iranians would acquire the ability to manufacture the materials compulsory for nuclear weapons with very little trouble.[125] Iran's reasoning for attaining a nuclear capacity is invalid to the West and Israel. They claim that Iran's large oil and natural gas reserves provide it with ample energy solutions. The West and Israel distrust Iran's motives and believe that they are attempting to develop nuclear weapons.

---

[123] Shahram Chubin, <u>Iran's Nuclear Ambitions</u> (Washington DC: Carnegie Endowment for International Peace, 2006), p24.

[124] Ibib, p24-25.

[125] Ibid.

1950s – 1979

The beginnings of the Iranian nuclear program can be traced back to 1959 with the purchase of a research reactor from the United States as part of the Atoms for Peace program which sought to limit the proliferation of nuclear weapons by controlling the manner in which nuclear technology was spreading.[126] In 1974, the Shah established the Atomic Energy Organization of Iran (AEOI) and precipitously began to negotiate for the acquisition of twenty three nuclear power plants which he sought to have in operational status by the mid 1990s.[127] Iran already had six nuclear power plants under contract with the French and the Germans by 1979.[128] Two German built nuclear plants at Bushehr were near completion at the time of the fall of the Shah.[129]

Iran's nuclear ambition under the Shah also included a rudimentary weapons research program even though Iran was a signatory member of the Nuclear Non-Proliferation Treaty since 1968.[130] It was believed to have been created with the aim of studying weapons designs and plutonium recovery from spent reactor fuel.[131]

---

[126] Congressional Research Service, Iran's Nuclear Program: Recent Developments (Washington DC: The Library of Congress, 2006), p1; see also Council on Foreign Relations, "Iran's Nuclear Program," (http://www.cfr.org/publication/16811/)

[127] Anthony H. Cordesman, Iran's Military Forces in Transition: Conventional Threats and Weapons of Mass Destruction (West Port: Praeger, 1999), p237, p366; see also Congressional Research Service, Developments, p1.

[128] Cordesman, Forces, p366; see also Council on Foreign Relations, "Iran's Nuclear Program,"

[129] Cordesman, Forces, p238, p366.

[130] Ibid; see also GlobalSecurity.org, "Nuclear Weapons – Iran," (http://www.globalsecurity.org/wmd/world/iran/nuke.htm); see also Council on Foreign Relations, "Iran's Nuclear Program,"

[131] Cordesman, Forces, p238, p366.

1979 – 1990s

By the time the revolutionary Khomeini government came to power, it wasted no time in cancelling the Shah's nuclear program, terminating the French and German contracts to build the agreed six nuclear power plants.[132] The decision not to pursue nuclear technology was however reversed as a result of the Iran-Iraq War.[133] A new nuclear research center was built in Esfahan in 1984.[134] That same year, work had resumed at the Bushehr plants which were badly damaged as a result of ongoing Iraqi bombing raids.[135] In 1987, Iran's nuclear weapons program was strengthened when it was announced that a uranium extraction plant would be established in the province of Yazd which had an abundance of uranium deposits.[136] That same year, Iran sought the help of foreign sources and accordingly signed a nuclear cooperation agreement with Pakistan and consequently and covertly benefited from the services of the AQ Khan network.[137] In addition, the Iranian government signed a formal nuclear research cooperation agreement with the People's Republic of China in 1990.[138]

The progress of the Iranian nuclear program had waned in the early 1990s as a result of declining oil revenues; a rapidly increasing population and war reconstruction efforts.[139] In addition to these

---

[132] Ibid, p367.

[133] Ibid; see also Chubin, Ambitions, p7.

[134] Cordesman, Forces, p368.

[135] Ibid; see also Roger Howard, Iran Oil: The New Middle East Challenge to America (London: I.B. Tauris, 2007), p142.

[136] Cordesman, Forces, p367.

[137] Ibid, p368; see also Congressional Research Service, Developments, p2; see also Takeyh, "Bomb," p51.

[138] Cordesman, Forces, p368.

[139] Chubin, Ambitions, p7.

setbacks, foreign sources were increasingly unwilling to provide Iran with nuclear assistance due to American opposition. For instance, Argentina – which had sold Iran uranium and had trained Iranian technicians in the late 1980s – was reluctant to aid the Iranian nuclear ambition, possibly as a reaction to US pressure.[140] China's nuclear assistance to the Islamic Republic had also decreased as its relations with the US improved.[141] When Germany, at the request of the Americans refused to continue its work on the Bushehr plant, Iran sought Russian assistance. It was announced in 1995 that Russia would agree to a deal to complete the reactors.[142] The Russian progress at Bushehr was snail-paced throughout the mid to late 1990s due to factors such as the incompatibility of Russian technology to the already existing German framework; vulnerabilities to seismic activity; and most importantly, the lack of prompt payments on the part of the Iranians.[143] The Bushehr plant was scheduled to be operational by 2007 however due to delays and a halt in construction, the completion date was pushed back to June 2009.[144]

2000 – 2009

The Iranian nuclear program was accelerated in the late 1990s early 2000s as work went into secretly constructing an underground uranium

---

[140] Cordesman, Forces, p369.

[141] Ibid, p371.

[142] Ibid, p373; see also Chubin, Ambitions, p7; Howard, Oil, p142; Council on Foreign Relations, "Iran's Nuclear Program,"

[143] Cordesman, Forces, p374; see also CBS News, "Iran Nuclear Chronology," (http://www.cbsnews.com/elements/2007/02/22/in_depth_world/timeline2504696.shtml)

[144] Howard, Oil, p142; see also VOAnews, "Iranian-Run Bushehr Plant has IAEA Oversight," (http://www.voanews.com/english/archive/2009-06/2009-06-10-voa60.cfm?CFID=261324429&CFTOKEN=16954979&jsessionid=88309314949620ce2a151e29325137861272)

enrichment complex in Natanz and a plutonium extraction facility in Arak.[145] In the summer of 2002, an Iranian dissident group – the National Council of Resistance of Iran (NCRI) – revealed information, largely believed to have been supplied by Israeli intelligence, pertaining to Iran's clandestine nuclear activities in both Natanz and Arak.[146] The covert nature in which these sites came to be was claimed to be in strict violation of the NPT and IAEA safeguards according to proponents of non-proliferation. Conversely, the Iranians claim that their actions were not an infringement of the safeguards dictated by the NPT which stated that the IAEA should be notified only when the intention to enrich uranium had been made.[147] Following inspections in June 2003, IAEA inspectors reported that Iran did in fact fail to comply with its obligations under the Safeguards Agreement of 1974.[148] Compliance failures included the withholding of construction and design details of the new facilities and failures to report processed and imported uranium, some dating back to 1991.[149]

The June 2003 inspections revealed that the Iranian nuclear program was much more advanced than had been originally suspected.[150] This prompted the US to seek movement of the issue to the UN Security Council, however the Europeans insisted on negotiating a way for Iran to halt its nuclear activities. Concurrently, the IAEA called on Iran to ensure full compliance and to suspend uranium enrichment.[151]

---

[145] Ibid, p143; see also Ali M. Ansari, Confronting Iran: The Failure of American Foreign Policy and the Root for Mistrust (London: Hurst & Company, 2006), p199.

[146] Ibid, p198; see also Congressional Research Service, Developments, p2; Howard, Oil, p21.

[147] Ansari, Failure, p200; see also Howard, Oil, p21.

[148] Council on Foreign Relations, "Iran's Nuclear Program,"

[149] Ibid.

[150] Howard, Oil, p21.

Iran was also told to ratify and implement the Additional Protocol – a mechanism designed to enhance snap inspections of Iranian nuclear facilities.[152]

In the autumn of 2003, Iran accepted the terms of the Tehran agreement with the EU-3 – France, the UK, and Germany – to suspend enrichment temporarily, pending the conclusion of negotiations, in addition to ratifying the Additional Protocol.[153] In exchange, the EU-3 agreed that it would recognize Iran's right to develop peaceful nuclear energy.[154] Within several months of this agreement, there were ongoing signs of sustained nuclear activity that called Iran's commitment into question.[155] This subsequently led to the 2004 Paris agreement which clarified the terms of the moratorium.[156] By March 2005, the Iranians were still adamant about continuing their enrichment process and declared that it would do so if negotiations did not progress.[157] That summer, the Iranians gave notice of their intention to recommence uranium enrichment despite the EU-3's offer of an incentives package in the event that they abandon their fuel cycle ambitions.[158] By January 2006, the IAEA confirmed reports that Iran had resumed uranium enrichment in Esfahan and in Natanz.[159] As a

---

[151] Chubin, Ambitions, p9.

[152] Ibid; see also Ansari, Failure, p203.

[153] Ibid, p9; Ibid, p205.

[154] Ansari, Failure, p205.

[155] Congressional Research Service, Developments, p5.

[156] Ibid.

[157] Ibid.

[158] Chubin, Ambitions, p9, p105.

[159] Reuters, "Timeline: Iran's Nuclear Program," (http://reuters.com/article/worldnews/idUSL0218278120071102?pageNumber=3&virtualBrandChannel=0;); see also Council on Foreign Relations, "Iran's Nuclear Program,"

result, the IAEA Board of Governors voted to report Iran to the UN Security Council which consequently led Iran to withdraw from the Additional Protocol.[160] The UN Security Council passed Resolution 1696 in July 2006 formally demanding Iran to suspend all nuclear activities by August 31st of that year, however instead of complying; the Iranians continued the enrichment process.[161] In December of that year, the UN Security Council voted to impose Resolution 1737 against the Islamic Republic which aimed at initiating a block on the sale and transfer of sensitive nuclear materials to and from Iran.[162] The expansion of Iran's uranium enrichment program prompted the Security Council to act again by imposing arms and financial sanctions in March 2007 (UNSC Resolution 1747).[163] Later that year, the US National Intelligence Estimate concluded that while it is probable that Iran halted its weapons program in the fall of 2003, the option to develop nuclear weapons has been kept.[164] In early 2008, the Permanent members of the UN Security Council in addition to Germany (P5+1), agreed to draft a third set of sanctions against Iran which was then passed in March 2008 (UNSC Resolution 1803) – the sanctions consist of bans on the trade of dual use goods in addition to travel restrictions on certain Iranian individuals.[165] In July 2008, the P5+1 offered the Iranian government a lucrative package of incentives however the Iranians failed to meet the group's deadline to accept the

---

[160] Ibid.

[161] Ibid.

[162] Ibid.

[163] Ibid.

[164] Council on Foreign Relations, "Iran's Nuclear Program,"

[165] CBS News, "Chronology,"

offer prompting the P5+1 to discuss a fourth round of sanctions against Iran.[166]

The year 2009 signalled the beginning of Barack Obama's presidency and with it came a shift in policy vis-à-vis Iran. The adoption of an engagement policy with Iran has given the Iranians another chance to negotiate over its nuclear program. The P5+1 improved the 2006 trade and diplomatic incentives package and removed preconditions that Tehran suspend its uranium enrichment before negotiations commence.[167] The Obama administration has also made goodwill overtures and indications that it is willing to engage in direct dialogue with Tehran, which it has not had in thirty years. The Iranian government has not budged on its refusal to halt enrichment and has responded to the Obama overtures by stating that it is waiting to see "real" policy shifts on part of the US before any talks begin.[168] At the 35th G8 Summit, President Obama stated that Iran would have until September 2009 to enter negotiations regarding its nuclear program or face possible "consequences" such as additional sanctions.[169]

As of April 9th 2009, which is the National Day of Nuclear Technology in Iran, the Islamic Republic of Iran has about 7,200 functioning centrifuges at the Natanz complex.[170] Iran is also constructing a commercial-scale plant nearby which will have fifty

---

[166] CNN, "Iran Confirms Nuclear Component Production,"
(http://edition.cnn.com/2008/WORLD/meast/08/29/iran.nuclear/index.html?eref=rss_world)

[167] Reuters, "El-Baradai Prods Iran Not to Ignore Obama Overtures,"
(http://www.reuters.com/article/worldNews/idUSTRE55E2UK20090615)

[168] Ibid.

[169] Reuters, "Obama Uses G8 Debut to Issue Warning to Iran,"
(http://www.reuters.com/article/GCA-Iran/idUSTRE56938J20090710)

[170] The New York Times, "Iran Has Centrifuge Capacity for Nuclear Arms, Report Says,"
(http://www.nytimes.com/2009/06/06/world/middleeast/06nuke.html)

thousand centrifuges in operation when fully functional.[171] Furthermore, as previously mentioned, construction on the Bushehr nuclear plant was finally completed in June 2009 – it is important to note however that the plant in Bushehr will be fully monitored by the IAEA and as such, the international community has no quarrel over its existence.[172] The US estimates that Iran will have enough fissile material to produce a nuclear device as early as 2011.[173]

Iranian motives for seeking nuclear weapons

The motivating factors required to seek nuclear weapons were presented in the second chapter. These causes of nuclear proliferation were explained by using the technological and bureaucratic imperative model; the international and domestic political model; and the national security model. These models will be used as a lens, focusing on the reasons why the regime in Tehran is adamant about developing a nuclear capability. Understanding Iran's nuclear ambition is crucial in identifying whether the international community's cause for concern is warranted. It will additionally provide the necessary data to devise a solution that could diffuse the situation.

Iran and the technological and bureaucratic imperative model

The emergence of a bureaucratic and scientific establishment possessing a parochial set of interests has undoubtedly helped guide Iran's nuclear program forward.[174] Ray Takeyh – a senior fellow at the

---

[171] CNN, "Iran Confirms,"

[172] VOAnews, "Iranian-Run Bushehr Plant has IAEA Oversight,"

[173] Congressional Research Service, Developments, p4.

[174] Takeyh, "Bomb," p60.

Council on Foreign Relations – expounds that under the auspices of the Iranian Revolutionary Guards Corps (IRGC), an entire assortment of organizations such as the Defense Industries Organization (DIO), university laboratories and a superfluity of companies, many of them owned by hardline clerics, have provided the thrust for Iran's expanding nuclear exertion.[175]

In addition, the technological savvy required to establish, develop and grow a nuclear program is rather remarkable. As Shahram Chubin points out, Iranians are proud of their efforts and achievements because they have broken into what they claim to be an exclusive "nuclear club".[176] These feelings of pride may help sustain and/or accelerate the current technological and bureaucratic drive present regarding the nuclear program.

The analysis of this motivational model within the Iranian context does not explain the reasons behind the genesis of Iran's nuclear ambition. It can be reasoned however that as the Iranian nuclear program progresses forward, technological and bureaucratic momentum sways in increasingly.

Iran and the international and domestic political model

As previously mentioned, the cause for nuclear proliferation can rest on a set of political variables. In this setting, a nuclear weapon is a policy option that can assist Iran pursue a foreign, and/or domestic objective.

---

[175] Ibid.

[176] Chubin, Ambitions, p25.

Iran and international and regional power and prestige

It can be argued that the mighty Persian Empire – which extended from the Mediterranean Sea to the Indus River – was the world's first superpower twenty five hundred years ago.[177] Iran's long and rich history serves as a reminder to Iranians that they have a rightful place amongst the great nations of the world. This contention can lead to the notion that the Iranians are nostalgic of once again being an important player on the world stage. The Shah of Iran originally initiated the nuclear program in the 1970s due to the belief that his country is great and that it ought to naturally be the dominant power in the region. Likewise, the clerical elite who have been at the helm of Iran since the 1979 Islamic Revolution vision the country as the dominant force in the neighbourhood. As Shahram Chubin notes: "Iran seeks to become the indispensable power in the Persian Gulf region, without which no regional policy can be implemented."[178]

The Iranians conspicuously want to have the ability to "flex their muscles" in the Persian Gulf region in order to satisfy their national interests. For example, Iran shares the Persian Gulf with members of the Gulf Cooperation Council (GCC) – Bahrain, Kuwait, Qatar, Oman, Saudi Arabia, and the United Arab Emirates (UAE) – with which it does not always see eye to eye.[179] Most of these Arab states have large Shiite minorities which have not been completely assimilated.[180] Many of the Arab rulers of the Persian Gulf States have forged strong defensive ties with the US.[181] The Persian Gulf States

---

[177] Marguerite Del Giudice, "Ancient Soul of Iran," National Geographic (August 2008), vol 214, no 2: p48.

[178] Ibid.

[179] Bahgat, "Islamic," p129.

[180] Ibid.

view Washington as their main guarantor of security against external threats. Some of them, such as Qatar and Bahrain, have even allowed American troops and facilities onto their soil.[182] Moreover, Tehran has an ongoing territorial dispute with the UAE over three islands – the Greater and Lesser Tunb, and Abu Mussa.[183] Additionally, the regime in Tehran is wary of post-Saddam Iraq. The two bordering countries continue to have a territorial dispute over the Shatt el-Arab waterway.[184] Baghdad also has close ties with Washington and as a result, the Iranians believe that they should be prepared for any outcome.[185]

Developments in the Persian Gulf are of incalculable importance to Iranian nuclear ambitions. From the Iranian perspective, the Persian Gulf is its most strategic arena, constituting its most reliable access to the international petroleum market.[186] This implies an ability to control the Persian Gulf militarily and deny its utilization by others if conflicts of interest arose.[187] Within these contexts, nuclear weapons would enhance Iran's regional status by giving it the means necessary to stand firm against its neighbours while also having the option to intimidate them if required.

Iran and domestic political and economic motivations

The absence of socio-political freedom coupled with a dismal economy makes it unsurprising that ordinary Iranians are lacking enthusiasm for

---

[181] Ibid.

[182] Ibid.

[183] Ibid.

[184] Ibid, p130.

[185] Ibid.

[186] Takeyh, "Bomb," p53.

[187] Eisenstadt, "Living," p126.

the clerical regime. The oppressive autocratic and theocratic government in Tehran is appealing only to a small fraction of the population: the families of martyrs from the Iran-Iraq War – who are taken care of by the regime; the impoverished classes who blame the West for Iran's troubles; the true believers – those aspiring to be the next generation of ruling elites; those within the circles of the ruling class; and those members of the Iranian special forces – the Basij, Ansar-e Hezbollah, the IRGC, and the Qods forces.[188] The rest of the population, seventy percent of whom are under the age of thirty, are disenchanted with the ruling mullahs.[189] This feeling has been heavily amplified as a result of the June 12th, 2009 Iranian presidential election, where many Iranians took to the streets in protest of what they believe to be vote rigging in favour of the incumbent president, Mahmoud Ahmadinejad. The massive crackdown led by the IRGC and the Basij forces has widened an already large rift between the people and the government. In this context, the development of a nuclear weapon can help repair the division between the majority of the populace and the ruling elite by diverting attention away from the concerns of the people and onto a national symbol of unity – a nuclear device.

Eighty percent of Iranians support the country's nuclear program.[190] As Chubin notes however, the debate has been warped by the regime, which has failed to release the facts or issues to public scrutiny.[191] The regime portrays the West's opposition to the nuclear program as a means of keeping Iran down.[192] The aim of this strategy

---

[188] Jared Cohen, "Iran's Young Opposition: Youth in Post-Revolutionary Iran," SAIS Review (Summer-Fall 2006), vol 26, no 2: p7-8.

[189] Ibid, p3.

[190] Chubin, Ambitions, p28.

[191] Ibid.

is to legitimize the regime domestically by garnering national sentiment.[193] Furthermore, Iran's international behaviour suggests that they welcome confrontation with the West. The way the hardliners in Tehran see it, confrontation would effectively rekindle popular support for the regime thus guaranteeing regime survival.[194] In other words, the development of nuclear weapons can be utilized as a "rallying round the flag" tactic, however only time will tell whether this tactic has any chance of success.

Economically speaking, an Iranian nuclear program could potentially save the regime much needed funds as an alternative to conventional arms spending. Iran's dismal stagnated economy which has double digit inflation and unemployment is in dire need of revitalization.[195] In this setting, moneys that would be normally used to fund the armed forces could be re-directed into the domestic economy.

Evidence shows that Iran's nuclear determination does not stem from a desire to improve economic benefits. Despite having a highly developed nuclear program, Iran continues to build-up its conventional forces using petro-earnings.[196] If the regime was sincere about stimulating the economy, it would divert those funds away from the defence industries. If Iran does cross the nuclear threshold however, it may decide to cut spending on conventional arms and rely on its newly acquired nuclear deterrent. Furthermore, Iran's continued defiance of international norms is driving away foreign direct

---

[192] Cohen, "Young," p9.

[193] Chubin, Ambitions, p28.

[194] Bahgat, "Islamic," p130; see also Takeyh, "Bomb," p56.

[195] Takeyh, "Bomb," p57.

[196] Howard, Oil, p139.

investments that are direly needed. Economic gains and relief have a minor role, if any, in aspiring Iran to develop nuclear weapons.

Although purely economic motivations may be lacking in Iran's nuclear ambitions, using the nuclear program as a bargaining chip is a plausible cause for keeping it running. The Agreed Frameworks between North Korea and the US in 1994 may have suggested to the Iranians that the nuclear issue can be used in exchange for incentives.[197] As mentioned earlier, the P5+1 have offered the Iranians a lucrative incentives package in exchange for cooperation and suspension on their nuclear program. The US has even broken with past policies and has offered to engage Iran diplomatically.

Iran and the national security model

Security concerns were argued as being the dominating factors for why states seek nuclear weapons. A nuclear device can add security assurances against adversaries by providing a deterrent that can potentially repel acts of aggression. In this context, a state would be inhibited from attacking the recent proliferator out of fears of a nuclear retaliation. The Iranian decision to re-launch the nuclear program in the midst of the Iran-Iraq War in the 1980s was strictly based on matters pertaining to national security. To better understand Iran's quest to achieve self-security, it is significant to identify and analyse each security concern that troubles the clerical regime. These security concerns can be categorically divided into the following:

- Iraq
- The need to build self-reliance

---

[197] Chubin, Ambitions, p20.

- Creating deterrence against the United States
- Creating deterrence against Israel

Iraq

Saddam Hussein long sought to have his country become the dominant power in the region. He wasted no time in attacking the vulnerable revolutionary Iran in 1980. Hussein's eagerness to settle the score over the disputed Shatt el-Arab waterway in addition to expelling Iran's revolutionary rhetoric led to an eight year conflict that resulted in approximately one million casualties.[198] The Iran-Iraq War has unquestionably shaped the regime's outlook on national security. For instance, the Iranians were surprised by Iraq's possession of surface to surface missiles; they were the recipients of Iraqi chemical weapons – while the international community turned a blind eye; and they had arms embargoes imposed on them which undeniably hindered their war fighting capability.[199] These actions against Iran were deeply scarring. As Takeyh reports, the memories of the war have led to cries of "never again".[200] Nuclear weapons in this setting serve as an insurance policy against future attacks.

The deposal of Saddam Hussein has decreased the Iraqi threat significantly but not entirely. As mentioned earlier, the dispute over the Shatt el-Arab waterway still exists. Additionally, Baghdad's close relationship with Washington is bothersome to the Iranians because should the domestic situation improve in Iraq, the US may use its close

---

[198] Gary G. Sick, Iran, Iraq, and the Legacy of War (New York: Palgrave Macmillan, 2004), p6.

[199] Chubin, Ambitions, p19; see also Eisenstadt, "Living," p125.

[200] Takeyh, "Bomb," p53.

ties with the Iraqis to establish a permanent American presence in the country – culturally, economically, and militarily.

The need to build self-reliance

Iran's sense of isolation during the Iran-Iraq War led to an emphasis on military self-reliance.[201] The Shah's Iran depended heavily on American arms imports. Due to an American led arms embargo following the 1979 US Embassy Hostage Crisis, spare parts were increasingly difficult to obtain as were replacements for losses, consequently obstructing revolutionary Iran's war efforts during the eight years of conflict. Furthermore, the international community's unsympathetic stance toward Iraq's use of chemical weapons led Iranians to believe that they were truly on their own. The Islamic Republic's sense of isolation is still apparent today. Tehran does not have a strategic partner. Even though Iran signed a defence pact with Syria in 2006, arguably Iran's closest friend, the pact does not pledge the defence of one by the other.[202]

As Chubin verbalizes:

> "The lessons of Iran's war with Iraq militate toward self-sufficiency in arms production; hedge against technological surprises – such as Hussein's use of surface to surface missiles; and do not rely on the international rules or community for any favours during times of crises.[203]

---

[201] Eisenstadt, "Living," p125.

[202] The Brookings Institution, "Defense Pact: Syria and Iran Revive Old Ghosts," (http://www.brookings.edu/opinions/2006/0704middleeast_saab.aspx)

[203] Chubin, Ambitions, p19.

Consequently, the Iranians developed their own domestic military industry with the objective of reducing its dependence on foreign arms imports; and minimizing the effect of future arms embargoes.[204] The Defence Industries Organization (DIO), the government's conglomerate in charge of the domestic defence industry, has the capacity to develop and sustain most of Iran's defence needs. As of 2008, Iran has the ability to produce artillery; personnel carriers; tanks; helicopters; short and medium range missiles; frigates; submarines and newly tested jet fighters.[205] Iran's domestic defence industry has also increased its arms exports over the years. UN Security Council resolution 1747 – passed in March 2007 – however prohibits Iran from continuing exporting arms.[206]

Creating deterrence against the United States

Tehran and Washington have been at odds with each other for nearly all of the Islamic Republic's existence. The events of September 11th 2001 have changed the American outlook on "rogue" states. The Bush administration's National Security Strategy did not differentiate between terrorists and those believed to be state sponsors of them. President George W. Bush's labelling of Iran as a member of the "axis of evil" in 2002 was seen as threatening by Tehran.[207] The American deployment of troops to Afghanistan in 2001 to overthrow the Taliban along with the invasion of Iraq in 2003 to topple Saddam Hussein, was a matter of great alarm to the Iranians. The US strategy to act pre-

---

[204] Eisenstadt, "Living," p125.

[205] Reuters, "How Big is Iran's Military?," (http://www.reuters.com/article/latestCrisis/idUSHAF238198)

[206] UN Security Council, "Security Council Toughens Sanctions Against Iran," (http://www.un.org/News/Press/docs/2007/sc8980.doc.htm)

[207] Chubin, Ambitions, p21.

emptively if necessary was worrisome to the clerical regime but what was more shocking to them was the swiftness with which the Americans overthrew their nemesis in Baghdad.[208] It took eight years for Iran and Iraq to conclude their war in a stalemate. It took twenty one days for the Americans to remove Saddam Hussein from power. Furthermore, the Iranians observed that Iraq's chemical and biological weapons capability failed to deter the Americans from using force, therefore Tehran may believe that only with a nuclear deterrent can it avert military confrontation with Washington.[209] It is also important to bear in mind that American interests in smaller tactical nuclear weapons have made the threats of nuclear usage against Iran a possibility, further reinforcing a need for a deterrent.[210]

The US presence in Afghanistan, Iraq and the Persian Gulf region makes it a possibility that Iran could be next on the hit list. The Bush administration was widely believed to have had adopted a policy of regime change for Iran and in 2003, the US Congress even appropriated funds to Iranian opposition groups.[211] President Obama's entry into the Oval Office has brought forth the policy aimed at engaging the Islamic Republic and avoiding the use of military force at all costs. The Obama overtures have not yet altered Iranian behaviour. As a result, it is safe to assume that Tehran still feels threatened by the US.

Taking the security issues discussed above into account makes it unsurprising that the government in Tehran is seeking security

---

[208] Takeyh, "Bomb," p54.

[209] Eisenstadt, "Living," p128.

[210] Chubin, Ambitions, p22.

[211] Chubin, Ambitions, p22.

assurances – which they believe nuclear weapons can provide. Even the Council on Foreign Relations concluded that Iran's nuclear ambitions are not reflective of an irrational set of strategic calculations.[212]

Creating deterrence against Israel

Iran's ambition to develop nuclear weapons did not originally stem from a desire to deter Israel.[213] The mullahs consider the state of Israel as being illegitimate. This belief in itself has not impelled Iran to pursue nuclear proliferation. These sentiments have however propelled Tehran to support pro-Palestinian groups against the Israelis.[214]

President Mahmood Ahmadinejad's rhetoric regarding Israel has been taken seriously by the international community, including Israel. As a result, Tel-Aviv is convinced that Iran would use a nuclear bomb against it were it to have one.[215] Some believe that the Iranian anti-Israeli rhetoric is regarded as being merely an attempt at mobilizing domestic and regional support against Israel and by association, the US.[216] Anti-Israeli sentiment within the clerical elite of Iran does not only revolve around anti-Zionism, but also to the arms asymmetry that exists in the region as a result of Israel's formidable armed forces.[217] Within this context, the Iranian nuclear ambition is sustained. Furthermore, the rapid progression of the Iranian nuclear program is being increasingly viewed as menacing by Israeli officials.

[212] Zbigniew Brzezinkski and R.M. Gates, Time for a New Approach (New York: Council on Foreign Relations, 2004).

[213] Takeyh, "Bomb," p53.

[214] Ibid.

[215] Dalia Dassa Kaye and F.M. Wehrey, "A Nuclear Iran: The Reactions of Neighbours," Survival (Summer 2007), vol 49, no 2: p112.

[216] Ibid.

[217] Bahgat, "Islamic," p129.

There are wide concerns that if diplomacy fails to halt Iran's nuclear program, Israel may launch a preemptive strike against Iranian nuclear facilities.[218] Such an attack would not be unprecedented. The Israelis pre-emptively destroyed Iraq's nuclear complex at Osirak in 1981, and allegedly struck a Syrian nuclear facility in 2007.[219]

Amid recent tensions, Iran has threatened to launch strikes against Tel-Aviv in the event of a US or Israeli attack.[220] In July 2009, the head of the IRGC, General Mohammad Ali Jafari, stated that should Israel strike Iran's nuclear facilities, Iran would reciprocate and strike Israel's nuclear facilities.[221] This heightened sense of tension could be a compelling cause to continue work on developing a nuclear capacity.

Summary

This section analyzed Iran's nuclear ambitions by using the technological and bureaucratic imperative model; the domestic political and economic model; and the national security model. All three models have had a part in explaining Iran's motivation to achieve nuclear proliferation.

It was revealed that due to security concerns, Iran's nuclear program was re-launched in the midst of the Iran-Iraq War. A technological and bureaucratic momentum sustained the rate of progression as did feelings of national pride and greatness. Iran's sense

---

[218] AFP, "Obama Says Israel Could Strike Iran," (http://afp.google.com/article/ALeqM5hSFLIDZBLLdXPlpUbrHbdCO00zGw)

[219] Eisenstadt, "Living," p128.

[220] Reuters, "Iran to Hit Tel-Aviv, US Ships if Attacked," (http://www.reuters.com/article/topNews/idUSLYO8285020080708?feedType=RSS&feedName=topNews)

[221] CNN, "Revolutionary Guard Leader: We Can Hit Israel's Nuclear Facilities," (http://www.cnn.com/2009/WORLD/meast/07/25/iran.israel.nuclear/index.html)

of isolation and abandonment reaffirmed its commitment to the nuclear program. The post September 11th 2001 American posture rang alarm bells within Tehran. Subsequent US intervention in neighbouring Iraq and Afghanistan has fuelled efforts to accelerate the nuclear program.

Currently, Iran's motivation to acquire nuclear weapons is based on the strategic security that it may be able to provide through nuclear deterrence. It is important to note that the decision to develop nuclear weapons has not been made and that Iran may be seeking to develop a nuclear option. It may also be using the nuclear program as a bargaining chip to gain benefits.

How would Iran behave with a nuclear weapon?

If Iran were to cross the nuclear threshold, would it behave with moderation or take on an aggressive posture?

Domestically, some believe that Iran's development of nuclear weapons would consolidate the regime's rule on the country and stamp out domestic dissent.[222] There is an uncertainty surrounding this possible outcome. The Soviet Union's massive nuclear arsenal did not act as a guarantor of regime security – the Union of Soviet Socialist Republics (USSR) collapsed despite its nuclear capability. The Soviet example shows that a nuclear weapon is not a tool used for domestic control.

Regionally, the greatest fear is that nuclear weapons will embolden Iran and lead the regime to act more aggressively by influencing the broader region.[223] With a nuclear weapon, the Iranians

---

[222] K. Timmerman, Countdown to Crisis: The Coming Nuclear Showdown with Iran (New York: Crown Forum, 2005), p304.

could become a rival to the US in the Persian Gulf region without having to fear being bullied around. As Kenneth R. Timmerman suggests, a nuclear Iran may behave much like it has in the past, but on steroids.[224] A nuclear capability may stimulate more radical elements to argue for a more ambitious set of policies.[225] Such policies can aggressively put an end to disputes over the Shatt el-Arab waterway with Iraq and over the Tunb and Abu Mussa islands in the Persian Gulf. They can also lead the Iranians to close off the Strait of Hormuz with more confidence in a time of crisis, affecting global oil prices. Iran may also support Shia activism more aggressively in the region.[226] Iran has not had the most impressive track record with regards to regional stability. Its attempt to destabilize the US in both Iraq and Afghanistan by meddling into their affairs in addition to its opposition to the Palestinian-Israeli peace process is proof of that.

Furthermore, as Chubin exclaims, there is cause for concern because the IRGC will likely be the custodian of the newly acquired nuclear capability, and they might see the WMD as an offensive weapon as opposed to a defensive one.[227] A nuclear device may also lead the Islamic Republic to use its proxies such as Hezbollah more deliberately while hiding under the shield of a nuclear deterrent.[228] The Islamic Republic may even extend a nuclear umbrella over its proxies

---

[223] Kaye and Wehrey, "Neighbours," p117.

[224] K.R. Timmerman, Countdown to Crisis: The Coming Nuclear Showdown with Iran (New York: Crown Forum, 2005), p304.

[225] Chubin, Ambitions, p54.

[226] Kaye and Wehrey, "Neighbours," p11.

[227] Ibid.

[228] Ibid.

and allies such as Syria. In a global context, Iran may act with more arrogance in bilateral and multilateral settings, hindering diplomacy.

It is important to note that there are some who believe that once Iran crosses the nuclear threshold, it will inevitably adopt a more pragmatic approach to international relations. In this setting, The Iranians will realize that their belligerent tactics are impractical in a nuclear world. This may lead Tehran to act with more caution and moderation.

As Eisenstadt puts it:

> "American, Soviet and Chinese experiences during the Cold War show that the destructive potential of nuclear weapons and the logic of deterrence moderate the behaviour of nuclear weapons states. They also incline their leaders towards caution thereby enhancing stability."[229]

---

[229] Eisenstadt, "Living," p132.

Chapter Six - Merging theory with practice: Iran and nuclear deterrence theory

In this chapter, the theoretical approaches to nuclear deterrence discussed in chapter three will be applied within an Iranian context. The supporting arguments of both proponents and skeptics of nuclear deterrence will be used to interpret Iran's contemporary nuclear program. The results ought to shed light on the limits, if any, of nuclear deterrence in a nuclear Iran era.

Nuclear Iran and the dissuasion of possible attack

According to nuclear deterrence theory, Iran's development of nuclear weapons would reduce the likelihood of it being the victim of a first strike more than it would if it were to remain a conventional military power. Assuming the US or Israel attack Iran with a tactical nuclear weapon, they would do so knowing that Iran would retaliate with a potentially devastating second strike. The Iranians are presently incapable of retaliating against the continental US but the Shahab-3 missile can easily reach Israel and US interests in the wider Middle East. More impressively, the Sajil-2 surface-to-surface missile has an approximate range of 2,000 kilometres which would put certain parts of Europe within reach.[230] Even without nuclear weapons, the Iranians have pledged to defend themselves against foreign aggression, therefore it is safe to assume that retaliation is a given in any scenario.[231]

---

[230] CNN, "Iran Tests New Surface-to-Surface Missile," (http://www.cnn.com/2009/WORLD/meast/05/20/iran.missile.test/index.html)

[231] Reuters, "Iran Tests Missiles, Vows to Hit Back if Attacked,"

In any case, nuclear deterrence should inhibit Iran's rivals such as the US or Israel from conducting a first strike due to the effects of Mutually Assured Destruction (MAD), thus dissuading possible attack.

Nuclear Iran and the likelihood of war

Proponents of nuclear proliferation can argue that the odds of a nuclear strike against another state are higher when a nuclear deterrent is absent. The American nuclear strikes on Nagasaki and Hiroshima in 1945 are testimony of this belief. Today, even though the use of nuclear weapons is widely regarded as taboo, the fact that the Americans sought to develop a low yield earth penetrating nuclear weapon – which could potentially be used to destroy Iran's deeply buried nuclear installations – makes it a reality that a nuclear weapons state has toyed with the idea of using a nuclear device on a conventional military state.[232]

Nuclear deterrence skeptics believe that although deterrence may prevent external attack, it does not stop the one deterring from being aggressive. If the proliferator is offensively motivated or acts in a manner which could be perceived as invasive, nuclear warfare could erupt. Conventional Iran has tendencies of being provocative at times. For instance, they conduct extensive war games every now and then – which could potentially be mistaken as a real attack. They sometimes act suspiciously at other times, such as when they captured British sailors in Iraqi waters in 2007.[233] Furthermore, the skeptics also

---

(http://www.reuters.com/article/topNews/idUSDAH9154220080709?feedType+RSS&feedName+topNews)

[232] BBC, "Mini-Nukes on US Agenda,"
(http://news.bbc.co.uk/1/hi/world/americas/3126141.stm)

[233] Washington Post, "Iran Seizes 15 Seamen," (http://www.washingtonpost.com/wp-dyn/content/article/2007/03/23/AR2007032300574.html)

believe that the chances of war erupting mathematically increase if Iran develops nuclear weapons. Iran's proliferation would add to the global stockpile increasing the quantitative odds of nuclear weapons being used accidentally or deliberately.

Proponents of deterrence theory assume that the state is a rational actor. It can be argued however that there exist elements within a state that are irrational. In an Iranian context for example, the regime loyalists – those chanting death to America and to Israel; members of the Special Forces such as the IRGC and the Basij characterize this type of behaviour. As mentioned earlier, nuclear deterrence is psychological, meaning that there is no guarantee that a state will use its nuclear forces rationally. The Islamic Republic of Iran's behaviour, although suspicious and provoking at times, has not crossed the threshold that divides rationality from irrationality, signifying a desire for self-preservation. If the regime collapses however, and a nuclear Iran finds itself in a temporary state of anarchy with fundamentalists such as the Basij out on the loose, then nuclear deterrence could be severely hindered.

Nuclear Iran, regional stability and the possibility of an arms race

The Islamic Republic of Iran has never attempted to invade another country but if it were to develop nuclear weapons, it may "flex its muscles" regionally and use conventional military force in the Persian Gulf region to achieve certain objectives such as securing its claim on the Shatt el-Arab waterway, the island of Abu Mussa and the Tunb Islands. A nuclear capable Iran may also confidently obstruct the Strait of Hormuz in the event of an international crisis. It is important to bear in mind that although Iran has bolstered its armed forces over the years, it has never acted invasively towards a neighbour, rhetoric aside. This may imply that a nuclear Iran may continue its rhetorical and diplomatic belligerence without crossing the fine line with actual physical confrontation. The Islamic Republic may use a nuclear device to its advantage by being diplomatically more assertive. It may aspire to be the region's China, where it may astray from international norms from time to time for its own benefit, without suffering the consequences from the international community.

The close proximity between Iran and its rivals further declines stability in the wider Middle East. Israel can for instance misinterpret an Iranian military exercise as being a nuclear attack. Close proximity and time constraints would make it difficult for the Israelis to establish a difference between a real attack and a military drill, consequently leading to a retaliatory strike against a misperceived threat. The likelihood of Iran launching a nuclear strike for this reason is even higher. Iran's sense of isolation and paranoia could lead to a rash decision to retaliate prematurely without differentiating the threat as being real or not.

Regional destabilization could possibly increase due to fears from Iran's neighbours as to what a nuclear Tehran may entail This may cause a domino effect and encourage Saudi Arabia, Egypt and potentially others to pursue nuclear proliferation, subsequently increasing tensions in the region.[234] Consequently an arms race may ignite, militarizing the wider Middle East.[235] Militarization in a volatile area such as the Middle East would be extremely destabilizing. Fears of an arms race erupting are strengthened when considering the growth

---

[234] Kaye and Wehrey, "Neighbours," p111.

[235] Ibid.

of Iran's domestic defence industry, as well as the rise of arms sales from the US to Saudi Arabia, Egypt, Israel and several other Persian Gulf states.[236] Additionally, a sense of pride and of not wanting to be left behind may encourage Egypt and Saudi Arabia to pursue nuclear proliferation.

Nuclear Iran and terrorism

The US labels Iran as the leading state sponsor of terrorism. Iran's elite military force, the IRGC, is designated by the US as a terrorist organization.[237] Iran's links to terrorism have always been ambiguous but the West is certain that Tehran was involved in the marine barracks bombing in Beirut in 1983 and the Khobar Tower bombings in 1996.[238] Iran's links to other US labelled terrorist groups such as Hezbollah and Hamas is a cause for concern to the West and Israel because they fear that if the Iranians develop nuclear weapons, they might share the technology or even extend their nuclear deterrent to them.

Considering that Iran has not shared chemical and biological weapons information or materials with terrorists suggests that this fear may be exaggerated. Then again, Iran's massive shipment of arms to Hezbollah; Hamas; and Iraqi insurgents makes it a possibility that nuclear technology and materials transfer could become a reality. The uncertainty surrounding Iran and terrorism is worrisome in itself. Another possibility to consider is that a nuclear weapon can be an authoritative device for control. In this context, a nuclear Islamic

---

[236] Reuters, "Iran's Military,"; see also Washington Post, "Iran Is Critical as US Unveils Arms Sales in the Middle East," (http://www.washingtonpost.com/wp-dyn/content/article/2007/07/30/AR2007073000623.html)

[237] AFP, "Senate Brands Guard as Terrorist Organization," (http://afp.google.com/article/ALeqM5hfpvyKJgNBecmX25n2WXOUPqVfpw)

[238] Chubin, Ambitions, p53

Republic of Iran would not want to share nuclear technology because it would jeopardize its new role as a nuclear power, and all the perks that may come with it.

Nuclear Iran and technical deficiencies

The Iranian's are proud of their scientific achievements with regard to their nuclear breakthroughs, but if the US has had technical difficulties with its nuclear arsenal then Iran could as well. Iran's opaque nuclear program increases the likelihood of technical deficiencies arising because external monitoring is limited and at times non-existent. Moreover, the opacity of Iran's nuclear activity has caused the UN to impose sanctions that could really technically hinder the nuclear program decreasing overall safety due to the absence of modern technologies and technical assistance. If Iran crosses the nuclear threshold in this context, the risks of a nuclear accident would be elevated. Additionally, Iran is prone to seismic activity which in turn can damage nuclear installations, potentially leading to the release of hazardous nuclear fallout into the region.

Nuclear Iran and organizational deficiencies

The Iranian nuclear program is currently under the umbrella of the IRGC.[239] As such, it is very likely that Tehran's nuclear weapons will likely be under their control.[240] As the guardian of the revolution, the IRGC is tasked with the preservation of the Islamic Republic and may resort to unconventional tactics in its mandate. The lack of civilian control and checks and balances over the IRGC, coupled with its belief

---

[239] Takeyh, "Bomb," p60.

[240] Council on Foreign Relations, "Iran's Revolutionary Guards," (http://www.cfr.org/publication/14324/)

in Islamic fundamentalism increase the chances of deterrence failure, for instance, in a time of public revolt. In this scenario, the IRGC may believe that the usage of nuclear weapons against whomever equates to the protection of the Islamic Republic. Over the years, the IRGC's influence over the Iranian government has grown exponentially, especially since President Ahmadinejad (a former Revolutionary Guard himself) took office in 2005. Many heads of departments and agencies are run by high ranking Revolutionary Guard members. In this context, the Revolutionary Guards may do what they deem necessary in order to ensure the continuance of their authority and influence over the Iranian government. The aggressive military nature of the IRGC makes their control over Iran's nuclear weapons quite worrisome and potentially unpredictable.

Nuclear Iran and political deficiencies

The regime in Tehran is politically deficient by nature. The regime is unpopular among the majority of the Iranian people, keeping the ruling elite on alert. They realize that the majority of Iranians would like to see them ousted from power. As it relates to nuclear weapons, if domestic revolt were to occur, the fanatical aspects of the regime may consider launching nuclear weapons against a rival. The argument here is that the ruling elite may hope to ignite nationalistic sentiment in the event of conflict with another nation, postponing their decline indefinitely. Another argument could be that the Iranian leaders would be willing to take the whole country down with them if they fear that their grip on power is slipping. These arguments, although not impossible, are also not likely to occur. The Iranian government has not acted rashly in its external relations and has not demonstrated suicidal tendencies.   Their moves, although unpredictable and provoking in the eyes of the West, have always seemed to have been calculated and well thought out.

Furthermore, the fact that Iran's nuclear program is opaque shows that the government in Tehran is aware of its international defiance. They have already violated IAEA safeguards and as such, the NPT itself, making them politically deficient internationally.   The opacity in Iran's nuclear development makes them untrustworthy with a nuclear weapon should it develop one.

Summary

In this chapter, theories of both skeptics and advocates of nuclear proliferation were applied within an Iranian context.   After careful examination, it was first revealed that should Iran go nuclear, it should in fact dissuade its rivals such as the US and Israel from launching a possible attack out of fear of a retaliatory second strike.

The likelihood of war erupting should remain at the status quo, once again, out of fear of realizing Mutually Assured Destruction. However, it was discussed that if the nuclear proliferator is offensively motivated, then the risks of war would increase. The Islamic Republic of Iran's calculated provocativeness serves as a reminder that it will not hesitate to defy international norms for its own benefit while keeping in mind the limit to which it can be belligerent. This in itself signals that the leaders in Tehran are self-aware and do not want to jeopardize their power by launching a first strike against a rival. It can be reasoned however, that the quantitative likelihood of war increases if Iran were to cross the nuclear threshold, due to the augmentation in the global stockpile of nuclear weapons. Furthermore, the risks of war may be elevated if irrational elements within Iran took control of its nuclear arsenal, for instance in a time of public revolt where the regime neared its collapse. The Revolutionary Guards or the Basij could take it upon themselves to do what they deemed necessary with nuclear weapons in a time of crisis.

Regional stability and the possibility of an arms race igniting would increase with a Nuclear Iran present. Tehran may decide to "flex its muscles" and become more assertive with its external relations. The close proximity between Iran and its neighbours would elevate the chances of a misinterpretation of a first strike possibly leading to warfare. Furthermore, if Iran does cross the nuclear threshold, it may spark a domino effect and lead Egypt and Saudi Arabia and potentially others towards nuclear proliferation consequently leading to an arms race/build up.

The connection between Iran and terrorist organizations is worrisome to the West and Israel. They fear the transfer of technology and/or materials from one to the other. Although this is a warranted cause for concern, the fact that the Islamic Republic has not shared chemical and biological weapons with terrorists suggests that Tehran is not interested in supplying them with WMDs. It may however, extend a nuclear deterrent, and/or support US labelled terrorist groups such as Hezbollah more aggressively, financially and through conventional arms transfer.

Deficiencies present in Iran may lead to an accidental or deliberate launch of a nuclear weapon. Possible technical deficiencies within the Iranian nuclear program may lead to a catastrophic nuclear accident. Iran's nuclear arsenal is likely to be controlled by the Revolutionary Guards which is a cause for concern in itself. Political deficiencies within Iran make it a possibility that domestic turmoil or fanatical elements within the regime may lead to a deterrence failure.

This analysis demonstrates that should Iran develop nuclear weaponry, deterrence failure is a realistic possibility. That is not to say that nuclear deterrence will fail, but that the Iranian government in concert with the international community ought to engage in order to decrease the likelihood of deterrence failure.

Chapter Seven - Preventing nuclear proliferation to Iran

In chapter four, methods of nuclear proliferation prevention were discussed. Such preventive measures would have the aim of coercing a state into circumventing its nuclear weapons program either willingly or forcefully. The measures discussed in chapter four will be used in the Iranian context in order to understand the avenues available in preventing Iran from developing a nuclear weapon.

Preventing nuclear proliferation to Iran through domestic changes

A change in the domestic political landscape may trigger a reversal in the decision to pursue nuclear weapons. As mentioned earlier in this book, the Iranian government is unpopular amongst the majority of its populace. Seventy percent of the population is under the age of thirty and many of them are looking beyond what the Islamic Republic can offer them. The student uprisings of 1999 and 2003 are examples demonstrating the strong urge that exists for social and political freedoms within Iran. The 2009 Iranian presidential election was an opportunity for the disenchanted Iranians to voice their discontent by voting for the candidate of their choice, namely Mir Hossein Mousavi, who they wanted to see replace incumbent president, Mahmoud Ahmadinejad. The result however, believed to be tainted, sent many Iranians to the streets in what was the largest mass demonstration since the 1979 Islamic revolution. These sentiments of ill will toward the Iranian government exemplify the reality that the government is in danger of subversion. If the Iranian government were to change into an international law abiding democratic state, either through revolt or reform, then the worry over Iranian nuclear ambitions may subside. That government may halt the nuclear program, or at the very least, fully comply with the international community in its nuclear activity.

Drastic governmental change does not need to occur for a roll back of nuclear policies. A change in attitude within the establishment of the Islamic Republic, more specifically, within the Office of the Supreme Spiritual Leader, may alter Iranian nuclear ambitions. The Supreme Leader has the final say in the affairs of the state and if that person decides that Iran is better off without nuclear weapons, then it may subdue the Iranian nuclear program, depending on how obedient the Revolutionary Guards feel.

Preventing nuclear proliferation to Iran through diplomacy

Preventing a country from acquiring nuclear weapons by diplomatic means consists of a strategy that revolves around dialogue and negotiations between those seeking prevention and the potential proliferator. In an Iranian context, the lack of diplomatic relations between Iran and the US renders direct dialogue difficult between the two. Despite the absence of diplomatic relations between Iran and the United States, the Swiss ambassador to Iran informed US officials in 2003 that an Iranian proposal for comprehensive talks with the United States had been reviewed and approved by Iranian Supreme Leader Ayatollah Ali Khamenei, then-President Mohammad Khatami and then foreign minister Kamal Kharrazi. In his communiqué to the State Department, the Swiss ambassador wrote that he had the clear impression that the regime in Tehran had a strong willingness to take on the problem with the United States with this initiative. A

"Roadmap" which described U.S. and Iranian aims for prospective negotiations was drawn up by the Iranian leadership and included issues such as an end to Iran's support for anti-Israeli militants, action against terrorist organizations on Iranian soil, acceptance of Israel's right to exist, and increased transparency of the nuclear program. Unfortunately, this "grand bargain" was not welcome by the Bush administration, which was riding high in confidence in the wake of the Iraqi invasion, and missed a golden opportunity to resolve the Iranian nuclear issue.

The June 2003 IAEA inspections revealed that the Iranian nuclear program was much more advanced than was originally thought, prompting the US to push the matter into the UN Security Council; however the Europeans insisted on negotiating a way for Iran to halt work on its nuclear program.[241]

In late 2003, Iran accepted the terms of the Tehran agreement with France, the UK, and Germany – the EU-3 – to suspend enrichment on a temporary basis, pending the conclusion of negotiations, in addition to ratifying the Additional Protocol.[242] In exchange, the EU-3 agreed that it would recognize Iran's right to develop peaceful nuclear energy.[243] Within several months of this agreement, there were ongoing signs of sustained nuclear activity that called Iran's commitment into question.[244] This subsequently led to the 2004 Paris agreement which clarified the terms of the moratorium.[245] By March

---

[241] Howard, Oil, p21.

[242] Ibid, p9; Ibid, p205.

[243] Ansari, Failure, p205.

[244] Congressional Research Service, Developments, p5.

[245] Ibid.

2005, the Iranians were still adamant about continuing their enrichment process and declared that it would do so if negotiations did not progress.[246] That summer, soon after newly elected President Mahmoud Ahmadinejad took office, the Iranians gave notice of their intention to recommence uranium enrichment despite the EU-3's offer of an incentives package in the event that they abandon their fuel cycle ambitions.[247] Negotiations more or less stood still in the coming years while this issue was moved to the UN Security Council.

By July 2008, the Bush administration softened its hard line position with regards to Iran and even contemplated opening a US interests section in Tehran.[248] That same month, the US joined in on the negotiations, along with China and Russia. Together with France, the UK, and Germany, the P5+1 offered the Iranian government a lucrative package of trade and diplomatic incentives. The Iranians however failed to meet the group's deadline to accept the offer prompting the P5+1 to discuss a fourth round of sanctions against Iran.[249]

The year 2009 signalled the beginning of Barack Obama's presidency and with it came a shift in policy with regards to Iran. The adoption of an engagement policy with Iran has given the Iranian leadership another opportunity to negotiate over its nuclear program. The P5+1 improved the 2006 trade and diplomatic incentives package and removed preconditions that Tehran suspend its uranium enrichment before negotiations begin.[250] The Obama administration has also made

---

[246] Ibid.

[247] Chubin, Ambitions, p9, p105.

[248] The Guardian, "US Plans to Station Diplomats in Iran for First Time Since 1979," (http://www.guardian.co.uk/world/2008/jul/17/usa.iran)

[249] CNN, "Iran Confirms Nuclear Component Production," (http://edition.cnn.com/2008/WORLD/meast/08/29/iran.nuclear/index.html?eref=rss_world)

goodwill overtures and indications that it is willing to engage in direct diplomatic dialogue with Tehran, which it has not done since the US Embassy Hostage Crisis of 1979. The Iranian government has not budged on its refusal to halt the enrichment of uranium. At the 35th G8 Summit in Italy, President Obama stated that Iran would have until September 2009 to enter negotiations regarding its nuclear program or face possible "consequences" such as additional sanctions.[251] This deadline however may be difficult to observe due to the 2009 Iranian presidential election fallout and may be pushed back as a result.

Diplomacy in this setting has yet to achieve its purpose of permanently suspending uranium enrichment and convincing Tehran to roll back its nuclear program, but with due diligence and consistency it may pay dividends. What diplomacy has done up to this point is thwart off military confrontation, at least for now. This in itself ought to be looked upon in a positive light. What diplomacy has also done is buy more time for the Iranian government to continue work on its nuclear program. All in all, for diplomacy to succeed, Iran's motivations for rigorously pursuing its nuclear program need to be addressed.

Preventing nuclear proliferation to Iran through non-proliferation regimes

The goal of the nuclear non-proliferation system is to discourage the spread of nuclear weapons through the usage of rules, protocols, norms, procedures and institutions that regulate the diffusion of nuclear

[250] Reuters, "El-Baradai Prods Iran Not to Ignore Obama Overtures," (http://www.reuters.com/article/worldNews/idUSTRE55E2UK20090615)

[251] Reuters, "Obama Uses G8 Debut to Issue Warning to Iran," (http://www.reuters.com/article/GCA-Iran/idUSTRE56938J20090710)

technology.[252] These agreements exist chiefly to ensure that nuclear technology is attained and employed explicitly for peaceful purposes while minimizing the incentives of nuclear weapons proliferation.[253] The major regimes of non-proliferation consist of the IAEA, and the NPT.

Iran is a signatory member of the NPT and as such, is subject to verifications by the IAEA. Even though Iran is a member of the NPT, under Article IV of the treaty, it has the alienable right to seek and develop peaceful nuclear energy through the transfer of equipment, materials, scientific and technological information with others. The problem however is that many of these transferred materials may also be of dual use, meaning that they can be diverted from a peaceful nuclear program to a weapons program with very little difficulty.

The other pillar of the global non-proliferation regime is the IAEA, whose role it is to ensure the peaceful use of nuclear energy by implementing a uniform set of safeguards to signatory members of the NPT. The IAEA carries out its mandate through inspections, auditing, accounting of inventory, and various surveillance techniques.

In the summer of 2002, Iran's heightened nuclear ambition was disclosed as the Natanz and Arak facilities were discovered. The covert nature in which these sites came to be was claimed to be in strict violation of the NPT and IAEA safeguards according to opponents of nuclear proliferation. Conversely, the Iranians claim that their actions were not an infringement of the safeguards dictated by the IAEA.[254] Under Article 42 of Iran's Safeguards Agreement with the IAEA, and

---

[252] Simpson and McGrew, International, p4; see also Sauer, Arms, p36.

[253] Simpson and McGrew, International, p4.

[254] Ansari, Failure, p200; see also Howard, Oil, p21.

according to the Subsidiary Arrangement, Iran is obligated to disclose nuclear activities six months prior to the introduction of nuclear material into a facility.[255] Therefore technically, the Iranians are correct in their argument that they were not obligated to notify the IAEA of the construction of its facilities.[256] Nevertheless, following inspections in June 2003, IAEA inspectors reported that Iran did in fact fail to comply with its obligations under the Safeguards Agreement of 1974.[257] Compliance failures included the non-disclosure of information pertaining to experiments involving nuclear material.[258] According to an IAEA report released in 2004, Iran failed to declare the following:

- Uranium imports: There was failure to report the purchase of natural uranium from China in 1991.[259]

- Uranium conversion: Iran did not report its use of imported uranium in conversion tests.[260]

- Uranium enrichment: The Iranians failed to inform the IAEA that it had used 1.9 kg of imported uranium to test centrifuges in 1999 and in 2002. Subsequently, there was also failure to report the production of enriched and depleted uranium.[261]

- Hidden sites: There was failure to notify the IAEA of the pilot enrichment facility at the Kalaye Electric Company Workshop,

---

[255] The Institute for Science and International Security, "Iran's NPT Violations – Numerous and Possibly On-Going?," p5. (http://www.isis-online.org/publications/iran/irannptviolations.pdf)

[256] Ibid.

[257] Council on Foreign Relations, "Iran's Nuclear Program,"

[258] ISIS, "Iran's NPT Violations"

[259] Ibid.

[260] Ibid.

[261] Ibid.

and the laser enrichment plant at the Tehran Nuclear Research Centre as well as in Lashkar Abad.[262]

- Laser isotope enrichment experiments: Iran was obligated to report that it had imported 50 kg of natural uranium metal in 1993 and that it used 8 kg of it for atomic vapour laser isotope separation at the Tehran Nuclear Research Centre between 1999 and 2000. It also used 22 kg of the metal at Lashkar Abad between 2002 and 2003.

- Plutonium experiments: Iran did not declare to the IAEA that it had separated plutonium from the irradiated targets of the uranium dioxide that it had produced between 1988 and 1993.

Despite these violations and as a result of negotiations with the EU-3, Iranian uranium enrichment had been suspended in late 2004 in accordance with the Paris Agreement, however their intent on resuming enrichment had been made clear by late 2005. In January 2006, the IAEA confirmed reports that Iran had in fact resumed uranium enrichment in Esfahan and in Natanz.[263] Consequently, the IAEA Board of Governors voted to report Iran to the UN Security Council. The IAEA has subsequently released reports pertaining to Iran's nuclear program, however the occasional Iranian reluctance to cooperate with the organization has made it difficult for the UN nuclear watchdog to comprehensively inspect, audit, and survey Iranian nuclear activities. Despite Iran's lack of total cooperation, the IAEA has been able to report its findings to the IAEA Board of Governors.

---

[262] Ibid.

[263] Reuters, "Timeline: Iran's Nuclear Program," (http://reuters.com/article/worldnews/idUSL0218278120071102?pageNumber=3&virtualBrandChannel=0;); see also Council on Foreign Relations, "Iran's Nuclear Program,"

August 2007 report

The August 2007 IAEA report stated that the agency has had the ability to verify the non-diversion of the declared nuclear materials at the enrichment facilities in Iran and has therefore concluded that it remains in peaceful usage.[264] The report also adds however that the IAEA remains unable to check certain aspects relevant to the scope and nature of Iran's nuclear program.[265]

The report also outlines a work plan agreed by the IAEA and the Islamic Republic of Iran on August 21st, 2007.[266] The work plan reflects agreement on "modalities for resolving the remaining safeguards implementation issues, including the long outstanding issues."[267] According to the plan, these modalities cover all remaining issues and the nuclear watchdog confirmed that there are no other remaining issues and ambiguities regarding Iran's past nuclear program and activities.[268] The IAEA report describes the work plan as a significant step forward; it also considers it imperative that Iran adheres to the time line defined therein and implements all the required safeguards and transparency measures, including those of the Additional Protocol.[269]

---

[264] IAEA, "Implementation of the NPT Safeguards Agreement in the Islamic Republic of Iran," (http://www.iaea.org/Publications/Documents/Board/2007/gov2007-48.pdf)

[265] Ibid.

[266] Ibid.

[267] Ibid.

[268] Ibid.

[269] Ibid.

November 2007 report

The report declared that on nine outstanding issues, Iran's statements are consistent with information available to the agency.[270] The IAEA also warned that its knowledge of Iran's nuclear work was decreasing due to the Iranians' refusal to implement the Additional Protocol.[271]

February 2008 report

In this report, the IAEA clarified many outstanding issues including the scope and nature of Iran's enrichment program.[272] One issue that remains unresolved is the extent to which Iran is studying the weaponization of its nuclear program.[273]

May 2008 report

The IAEA has been able to verify the non-diversion of declared nuclear material in Iran.[274] The IAEA requested access to centrifuge manufacturing sites, but the Iranians refused.[275] The agency has not detected any evidence of actual design or manufacture of nuclear weapons or components.[276]

---

[270] IAEA, "November 2007 Report: Implementation of the NPT Safeguards Agreement and Relevant Provisions of Security Council Resolutions 1737 and 1747 in the Islamic Republic of Iran,"
(http://www.iaea.org/Publications/Documents/Board/2007/gov2007-58.pdf)

[271] Ibid.

[272] IAEA, "Latest Iran Safeguards Report Circulated to IAEA Board,"
(http://www.iaea.org/NewsCenter/News/2008/iranreport0208.html)

[273] Ibid.

[274] IAEA, "May 2008 Report: Implementation of the NPT Safeguards Agreement and Relevant Provisions of Security Council Resolutions 1737, 1747 and 1803 in the Islamic Republic of Iran,"
(http://www.iaea.org/Publications/Documents/Board/2008/gov2008-15.pdf)

[275] Ibid.

September 2008 report

Iran continued to provide the IAEA with access to declared nuclear material and activities.[277] Activities confirmed to operate under safeguards.[278] There is no evidence of weapons diversion; however the IAEA is unable to verify the true nature of the declared peaceful program without the Additional Protocol.[279]

Analysis

The IAEA has been able to fulfill its mandate in an Iranian context. It has access to Iran's declared nuclear activities. It does not have access to anything that may be clandestine however, if such facilities even exist, and consequently is not able to prove a parallel nuclear program in Iran and can not gauge Iranian intent with regards to nuclear weapons development.

It is important to note that Iran's nuclear activities are closely scrutinized by the IAEA and that weapons diversion would be instantly verifiable due to broken seals and video recordings captured by installed cameras at the installations. The IAEA is certain that it has not located any evidence suggesting that weaponization of the nuclear program is in progress. It seems as if the bulk of Iran's IAEA

---

[276] Ibid.

[277] IAEA, "September 2008 Report: Implementation of the NPT Safeguards Agreement and Relevant Provisions of Security Council Resolutions 1737, 1747 and 1803 in the Islamic Republic of Iran," (http://www.isis-online.org/publications/iran/IAEA_Iran_Report_15September2008.pdf)

[278] Ibid.

[279] Ibid.

violations occurred prior to 2002-2003. It is undisputable that since the revelations of the facilities in Natanz and Arak in 2002, Iran has been the most heavily inspected country in the world by the IAEA.

Further, the NPT has done exactly what it was designed to do, and that is to allow Iran attain nuclear materials and technology for a peaceful program, which is permitted under Article IV of the treaty. The NPT is unable to prevent the diversion of dual use technology as it was never designed to do so. An amendment to the NPT may fill in this loop hole. Furthermore, Iran can easily withdraw from the treaty in accordance with Article X of the Treaty.[280] If that occurs, the IAEA will no longer have the ability to inspect the declared nuclear installations in Iran.

Preventing the proliferation of nuclear weapons to Iran through the use of force

If negotiations to halt a state's nuclear weapons program fail, members of the international community may pursue forceful action in order to coerce the proliferator to roll its nuclear policies back. As it was previously mentioned in chapter three, a preventive strike is a state's forceful response to a long term threat.

Within an Iranian context, preventive measures can easily become a reality. The Israelis feel threatened by Iran's nuclear program, especially since President Ahmadinejad took office in 2005. They believe that President Ahmadinejad's rhetoric towards Israel reflects the actuality of an Iranian nuclear weapon possibly heading

---

[280] United Nations, "NPT Treaty," (http://www.un.org/events/npt2005/npttreaty.html)

their way. As a result, they have reiterated time after time that "all options remain on the table" when considering the Iranian nuclear threat. It would seem that the Israelis are preparing for the worst by conducting war game scenarios. They have sent warships through the Suez Canal; tested their Arrow antiballistic missile defence system; and even conducted nationwide emergency drills.[281] An Israeli preventive strike against Iranian sites would not be unprecedented. The Israelis struck a nuclear facility in Iraq in 1981 and again in Syria in 2007. The US has also refused to take military action "off the table". Even though the US' policies towards Tehran have shifted significantly towards diplomatically engaging Iran, the option to intervene forcefully remains.

Preventive strikes against the Islamic Republic of Iran would undoubtedly be destabilizing to the wider Middle East region. Firstly, the Iranians have all but guaranteed a military response to Israel and potentially US interests in the area should their nuclear facilities come under attack. Although Iran's defensive capabilities are not as technologically advanced as that of the Israelis or Americans, they are still formidable and a cause for concern should war erupt. It could potentially be devastating to the US as they have large numbers of troops and personnel in both Iraq and Afghanistan, which neighbour Iran. The Americans also have military bases in the Persian Gulf, namely in Qatar and Bahrain, both in close proximity to Iran and its armed forces. Preventive strikes against Iran would be destabilizing for Israel. Aside from the possibility of war breaking between Tehran and Tel Aviv, Hezbollah and other groups and/or individuals sympathetic to

---

[281] The Wall Street Journal, "Conflict is Inevitable Unless the West Moves Quickly to Stop a Nuclear Iran," August 31st, 2009.

the Iranians may launch attacks against Israel themselves. War with Iran would be economically devastating as well, having a global impact. An enormous amount of fossil fuel and liquid natural gas crosses the Strait of Hormuz on a daily basis. Tehran may deploy mines to block the flow of shipment through the narrow water passageway, causing the global price of petroleum based products, including oil, to skyrocket. In the worst of scenarios, a preventive strike on Iran may instigate the largest global conflict since the Second World War. Say Israel strikes Iran; the Iranians may retaliate against Israel and maybe even the US. The US would then be forced to enter the conflict, potentially prompting others such as Russia and China to get involved. The cost benefit of a military strike against Iran is minimal. There is no guarantee that Iran would simply abandon its nuclear program after being attacked, it may at best set the program back a few years. Strikes against Iran would also be detrimental to the democratic movement that exists in the country. Nationalistic and patriotic sentiments may temporarily unite the Iranian populace against the foreign enemy and give the ruling establishment a lifeline. Conversely, it may have the opposite effect, giving the democratic movement a chance to topple the leadership. It is difficult to gauge the internal affairs of Iran in the event of war; it is however safe to assume that what ever action is taken by the populace will be driven largely by pride.

Chapter Eight - Conclusion

It has been discussed that nuclear proliferation may be guided by technological and bureaucratic imperatives; international and domestic political factors; and predominantly, reasons pertaining to national security. The need to obtain nuclear weapons for security purposes rests on its ability to be a strategic deterrent.

It was revealed that due to security concerns, Iran's nuclear program was re-launched in the midst of the Iran-Iraq War. A technological and bureaucratic momentum sustained the rate of progression as did feelings of national pride and greatness. Iran's sense of isolation and abandonment reaffirmed its decision to pursue the nuclear program. September 11th 2001 aggressively transformed American foreign policy, ringing alarm bells in Tehran. The subsequent US intervention in neighbouring Iraq and Afghanistan further fuelled efforts to accelerate the nuclear program.

Iran's motivation to acquire a nuclear capability is based on the strategic security that it can provide through nuclear deterrence. It will also make them indispensable in the Persian Gulf region, potentially giving them the ability to have a say on all matters of the area. It is imperative to single out that the decision to develop nuclear weapons has not officially been made and that no evidence exists that would suggest weapons diversion. If the Iranians are being truthful about developing peaceful nuclear energy, their desire to have the fuel cycle would give them a nuclear option by default.

Nuclear deterrence theory rests on what has been coined as Mutually Assured Destruction, meaning that an adversary ought to be made aware that a first strike against it would be foolish due to the punishing second strike blow that may be reciprocated. It has been discussed that proponents of nuclear deterrence, namely Waltz, believe that the spread of nuclear weapons is beneficial to global stability. They refer to the fact that it has been proven to work during the Cold War. Conversely, the skeptics of nuclear deterrence believe that more nuclear weapons would be detrimental to the stability of the international system.

If Iran were to cross the nuclear threshold, it may adopt an aggressive posture. Domestically, some believe that Iran's development of nuclear weapons would consolidate the regime's rule on the country and stamp out domestic dissent.[282] Regionally, the greatest fear is that nuclear weapons will embolden Iran and lead the regime to act more invasively by influencing the broader region.[283] With a nuclear weapon, the Islamic Republic of Iran could become a rival to the US in the Persian Gulf region without having to fear being bullied around. A nuclear capability may stimulate more radical elements of the regime to argue for a more ambitious set of policies.[284] Such policies can aggressively put an end to disputes over the Shatt el-Arab waterway with Iraq and over the Tunb and Abu Mussa islands in the Persian Gulf. Nuclear weapons may also lead Iran to support Shia activism more aggressively.[285]

A nuclear device may also lead the Islamic Republic to use their proxies such as Hezbollah more deliberately while hiding under

---

[282] Timmerman, Showdown, p304.

[283] Kaye and Wehrey, "Neighbours," p117.

[284] Chubin, Ambitions, p54.

[285] Kaye and Wehrey, "Neighbours," p118.

the shield of a nuclear deterrent.[286]   The Islamic Republic may even extend a nuclear umbrella over its proxies and allies such as Syria. Iran's development of nuclear weapons would surely embolden it.

Should the international community be worried?

If Iran were to develop nuclear weapons, nuclear deterrence theory ought to work in preventing another state such as the US or Israel from launching a first strike due to the Iranian capacity to launch a retaliatory second strike.   As the prominent proponent of nuclear deterrence exclaims, nuclear deterrence has been proven to work during the Cold War between the US and the Soviets, therefore it should work in an Iranian context.

The likelihood of war erupting should remain at the status quo out of fear of realizing Mutually Assured Destruction. It was revealed however that although nuclear deterrence may be effective in preventing external aggression, it is susceptible to failures emanating from within. The Islamic Republic of Iran's calculated provocativeness serves as a reminder that it will not hesitate to defy international norms for its own benefit while bearing in mind the limit to which it can be belligerent. This in itself signals that the leaders in Tehran are self-aware and do not want to jeopardize their power by launching a first strike against a rival. It can be reasoned however, that the quantitative likelihood of war increases if Iran were to cross the nuclear threshold, due to the augmentation in the global stockpile of nuclear weapons. Furthermore, the risks of war may be elevated if irrational elements within Iran took control of its nuclear arsenal, for instance in a time of

---

[286] Ibid.

public revolt where the regime neared its collapse. The Revolutionary Guards or the Basij could take it upon themselves to do what they deemed necessary with nuclear weapons in a time of crisis.

Regional stability and the possibility of an arms race igniting would increase with a Nuclear Iran present. Tehran may decide to "flex its muscles" and become more assertive with its external relations. The close proximity between Iran and its neighbours would elevate the chances of a misinterpretation of a first strike possibly leading to warfare. Furthermore, if Iran does cross the nuclear threshold, it may spark a cascade of nuclear proliferation in the region, leading Egypt, Saudi Arabia and potentially others towards nuclear weapons. Further proliferation in the region may also spark an arms race/build up between Iran and its neighbours much like that of the US and the Soviet Union during the Cold War.

In the post September 11th era, fears of linkages between states and terrorists are front and centre. The Islamic Republic of Iran has been referred to as the leading state sponsor of terrorism. The connection between Iran and terrorist organizations is worrisome to the West and Israel. They fear the transfer of technology and/or materials from one to the other. Although this is a legitimate cause for concern, the fact that the Islamic Republic has not shared chemical and biological weapons with terrorists suggests that Tehran is not interested in supplying them with WMDs. It may however, extend a nuclear deterrent, and/or support US labelled terrorist groups such as Hezbollah more aggressively, financially and through conventional arms transfer.

Deficiencies present in Iran may lead to an accidental or deliberate launch of a nuclear weapon. Possible technical deficiencies within the Iranian nuclear establishment may lead to a catastrophic nuclear accident. Iran's nuclear arsenal is likely to be controlled by the Revolutionary Guards which is a cause for concern in itself. Political deficiencies within Iran make it a possibility that domestic turmoil or fanatical elements within the regime may lead to a deterrence failure.

Should Iran develop atomic weaponry, deterrence failure will be a realistic possibility, thus the international community does have a warranted cause for concern should the Islamic Republic of Iran go nuclear.

Policy options

In order to compel the Iranians to abandon their nuclear ambitions, or at the very least their desire to possess the fuel cycle, their motivations for seeking nuclear proliferation need to be addressed. Their security concerns, their desire to have a voice in the region, national pride, and their legitimate energy needs are the primary reasons why they have a nuclear program.

Considering that the US is a major security concern to Iran it would have to play a central role in defusing the Iranian nuclear saga. The US must engage the regime directly and open a dialogue with Tehran. The aim would be to persuade the Iranians to halt their nuclear activities by offering them a balance of carrots and sticks. The US could lift the freeze on Iranian assets and ease bilateral economic sanctions in addition to providing security guarantees.[287] A regional security forum could then be established to address Iran's regional security concerns. Iran's application to the WTO could also be reviewed. Steps could also be taken to fully normalize bilateral

---

[287] Tekeyh, "Bomb," p61.

relations between Washington and Tehran. Improving relations with the US would improve Iran's relations with the European Union (EU) and the majority of the international community by association. President Barack Obama has already signalled that he is willing to diplomatically engage the leadership in Tehran.

In exchange for the American offer, the Iranians would have to reduce the momentum of their nuclear program, accept the Additional Protocol and allow full IAEA inspections. If the Iranians accept, than it would slowly but surely be reintegrated into the international community but should it reject the offer or continue to delay negotiations until it eventually crosses the nuclear threshold, then at least efforts were made at defusing the matter. Failed efforts would likely lead the West to impose stringent unilateral sanctions on Iran as tough UN Security Council sanctions would likely be opposed by Russia and China. These sanctions could either lead the regime in Tehran to roll its nuclear policies back and work cooperatively with the West or if strict enough, it could help fuel domestic opposition against the clerical regime.

The mistrust in Iran can be subdued if the West, most notably the US, engages Iran in a positive and constructive fashion in order to signal to the Iranians that their national security will not be compromised and that they have a legitimate role to play in the wider Middle East.

The Iranians want to be welcomed into the international community but only as they are. Changing itself, by foregoing the fuel cycle, or the nuclear program altogether, to appease the West and Israel is seen by the leadership as weakness. Furthermore, Iran's quarrel with Israel will unlikely end in the public square as it gives the leaders in

Tehran a target for its frustrations. It allows the leaders to rally the regime loyalists, who will in turn protect the regime from demise, which is also why Israel's existence is important to the regime.

BIBLIOGRAPHY

Books

Ansari, A.M., Confronting Iran: The Failure of American Foreign Policy and the Root for Mistrust, London: Hurst & Company, 2006.

Bader, William B., The United States and the Spread of Nuclear Weapons, New York: Pegasus, 1968.

Bailey, Kathleen C., Doomsday Weapons in the Hands of Many: The Arms Control Challenge of the 1990s, Urbana: University of Illinois Press, 1991.

Blix, Hans, "Foreword," in Joseph F. Pilat and Robert E Pendley, eds., Beyond 1995: The Future of the NPT Regime, New York: Plenum Press, 1990.

Brzezinkski, Zbigniew, and Gates, R.M., Time for a New Approach, New York: Council on Foreign Relations, 2004.

Carnesale, A., Doty, P., Hoffman, S., Huntington, S.P., Nye, J.S., and Sagan, S., Living with Nuclear Weapons, Cambridge: Harvard University Press, 1983.

Chubin, Shahram, Iran's Nuclear Ambitions, Washington DC: Carnegie Endowment for International Peace, 2006.

Clapp, P., and Halperin, M., Bureaucratic Politics and Foreign Policy, Washington DC: Brookings Institution Press, 2007.

Congressional Research Service, Iran's Nuclear Program: Recent Developments, Washington DC: The Library of Congress, 2006.

Cordesman, Anthony H., Iran's Military Forces in Transition: Conventional Threats and Weapons of Mass Destruction, West Port: Praeger, 1999.

Hagerty, Devin T., The Consequences of Nuclear Proliferation: Lessons from South Asia, Cambridge: MIT Press, 1998.

Howard, Roger, Iran Oil: The New Middle East Challenge to America, London: I.B. Tauris, 2007.

Meyer, Stephen M., The Dynamics of Nuclear Proliferation, Chicago: University of Chicago Press, 1984.

Reiss, Mitchell, Without the Bomb: The Politics of Nuclear Non-proliferation, New York: Columbia University Press, 1988.

Sagan, S.D., and Waltz, K.N., The Spread of Nuclear Weapons, New York: W.W. Norton & Company, 2003.

Sauer, Tom, Nuclear Arms Control: Nuclear Deterrence in the Post Cold War Period, London: Macmillan Press, 1998.

Sick, Gary G., Iran, Iraq, and the Legacy of War, New York: Palgrave Macmillan, 2004.

Simpson, John, and McGrew, A.G., The International Nuclear Non-proliferation System: Challenges and Choices, London: Macmillan Press, 1984.

Smith, Derek D., Deterring America, Cambridge: Cambridge University Press, 2006.

Timmerman, K., Countdown to Crisis: The Coming Nuclear Showdown with Iran, New York: Crown Forum, 2005.

Journals

Bahgat, Gawdat, "Nuclear Proliferation: The Islamic Republic of Iran," International Studies Perspective (2006), no 7: p124-136.

Bueno de Mesquite, B., and Riker, W.H., "An Assessment of the Merits of Selective Nuclear Proliferation," Journal of Conflict Resolution (June 1982), vol 26, no 2.

Bull, H., "Rethinking Non-proliferation," International Affairs (April 1975), vol 51, no 2.

Cohen, J., "Iran's Young Opposition: Youth in Post-Revolutionary Iran," SAIS Review (Summer-Fall 2006), vol 26, no 2: p1-15.

Chubin, Shahram, and Green, J.D., "Engaging Iran: A US Strategy," Survival (Autumn 1998), vol 40, no 3: p153-169.

Del Giudice, M., "Ancient Soul of Iran," National Geographic (August 2008), vol 214, no 2: p34-67.

Eisenstadt, M., "Living with a Nuclear Iran?," Survival (Autumn 1999), vol 41, no 3: p124-148.

Kaye, D.D., and Wehrey, F.M., "A Nuclear Iran: The Reactions of Neighbours," Survival (Summer 2007), vol 49, no 2: p111-128.

Mearsheimer, J.J., "Back to the Future: Instability in Europe after the Cold War," International Security (Summer 1990), vol 15, no 1.

Nye, J.S., "Maintaining a Non-proliferation Regime," International Organization (Winter 1981), vol 35, no 1.

Nye, J.S., "NPT: The Logic of Inequality," <u>Foreign Policy</u> (Summer 1985), no 59.

Takeyh, R., "Iran Builds the Bomb," <u>Survival</u> (Winter 2004-2005), vol 46, no 4: p51-64.

Thayer, B.A., "The Causes of Nuclear Proliferation and the Utility of the Non-proliferation Regime," <u>Security Studies</u> (Spring 1995), vol 4, no 3: p463-519.

Media sources; policy think tanks; research institutes; government and international organization resources

AFP, "Iran has up to 6,000 Uranium Centrifuges: Ahmadinejad," 27 July 2008.

AFP, "Obama Says Israel Could Strike Iran,"
http://afp.google.com/article/ALeqM5hSFLIDZBLLdXPlpUbrHbdCO00zGw

AFP, "Senate Brands Guard as Terrorist Organization,"
http://afp.google.com/article/ALeqM5hfpvyKJgNBecmX25n2WXOUPqVfpw

American Society of International Law, "North Korea's Withdrawal from the NPT," http://www.asil.org/insights/insigh96.htm

BBC, "Libya's Secret WMD,"
http://news.bbc.co.uk/1/hi/world/middle_east/3336109.stm

BBC, "Mini-Nukes on US Agenda,"
http://news.bbc.co.uk/1/hi/world/americas/3126141.stm

BBC, "Pros and Cons of the NPT,"
http://news.bbc.co.uk/1/hi/world/americas/4491003.stm

CBS News, "Iran Nuclear Chronology," http://www.cbsnews.com/elements/2007/02/22/in_depth_world/timeline2504696.shtml

Council on Foreign Relations, "Iran's Nuclear Program," http://www.cfr.org/publication/16811/

Council on Foreign Relations, "Iran's Revolutionary Guards," http://www.cfr.org/publication/14324/

Council on Foreign Relations, "The Six Party Talks on North Korea's Nuclear Program," http://www.cfr.org/publication/13593/

CNN, "Air Force Investigates Mistaken Transport of Nuclear Warheads," http://edition.cnn.com/2007/US/09/05/loose.nukes/index.html

CNN, "Iran Confirms Nuclear Component Production," http://edition.cnn.com/2008/WORLD/meast/08/29/iran.nuclear/index.html?eref=rss_world

CNN, "Revolutionary Guards Leader: We Can Hit Israel's Nuclear Facilities," http://www.cnn.com/2009/WORLD/meast/07/25/iran.israel.nuclear/index.html

CNN, "Iran Tests New Surface-to-Surface Missile," http://www.cnn.com/2009/WORLD/meast/05/20/iran.missile.test/index.html

Federation of American Scientists, "Nuclear Weapons in the Former Soviet Union," http://www.fas.org/spp/starwars/crs/91-144.htm

GlobalSecurity.org, "Nuclear Weapons – Iran,"
http://www.globalsecurity.org/wmd/world/iran/nuke.htm

IAEA, "Implementation of the NPT Safeguards Agreement in the Islamic Republic of Iran,"

http://www.iaea.org/Publications/Documents/Board/2007/gov2007-48.pdf

IAEA, "November 2007 Report: Implementation of the NPT Safeguards Agreement and Relevant Provisions of Security Council Resolutions 1737 and 1747 in the Islamic Republic of Iran,"

http://www.iaea.org/Publications/Documents/Board/2007/gov2007-58.pdf

IAEA, "May 2008 Report: Implementation of the NPT Safeguards Agreement and Relevant Provisions of Security Council Resolutions 1737, 1747 and 1803 in the Islamic Republic of Iran,"

http://www.iaea.org/Publications/Documents/Board/2008/gov2008-15.pdf

IAEA, "September 2008 Report: Implementation of the NPT Safeguards Agreement and Relevant Provisions of Security Council Resolutions 1737, 1747 and 1803 in the Islamic Republic of Iran,"

http://www.isis-online.org/publications/iran/IAEA_Iran_Report_15September2008.pdf

IAEA, "Latest Iran Safeguards Report Circulated to IAEA Board,"

http://www.iaea.org/NewsCenter/News/2008/iranreport0208.html

Nuclear Threat Initiative, "Iranian Nuclear Sites,"
http://www.nti.org/e_research/profiles_pdfs/Iran/iran_nuclear_sites.pdf

Reuters, "El-Baradai Prods Iran Not to Ignore Obama Overtures,"
http://www.reuters.com/article/worldNews/idUSTRE55E2UK2009061
5

Reuters, "How Big is Iran's Military?,"
http://www.reuters.com/article/latestCrisis/idUSHAF238198

Reuters, "Iran Tests Missiles, Vows to Hit Back if Attacked,"
http://www.reuters.com/article/topNews/idUSDAH9154220080709?fee
dType+RSS&feedName+topNews

Reuters, "Iran to Hit Tel-Aviv, US Ships if Attacked,"
http://www.reuters.com/article/topNews/idUSLYO8285020080708?fee
dType=RSS&feedName=topNews

Reuters, "Obama Uses G8 Debut to Issue Warning to Iran,"
http://www.reuters.com/article/GCA-Iran/idUSTRE56938J20090710

Reuters, "Timeline: Iran's Nuclear Program,"
http://reuters.com/article/worldnews/idUSL0218278120071102?pageN
umber=3&virtualBrandChannel=0

The Brookings Institution, "Defense Pact: Syria and Iran Revive Old
Ghosts,"
http://www.brookings.edu/opinions/2006/0704middleeast_saab.aspx

The Guardian, "US Plans to Station Diplomats in Iran for First Time
Since 1979,"
http://www.guardian.co.uk/world/2008/jul/17/usa.iran

The Institute for Science and International Security, "Iran's NPT
Violations – Numerous and Possibly On-Going?,"
http://www.isis-online.org/publications/iran/irannptviolations.pdf

The New York Times, "U.S. Says Iran Ended Atomic Arms Work,"
http://www.nytimes.com/2007/12/03/world/middleeast/03cnd-iran.html

The New York Times, "Iran Has Centrifuge for Nuclear Arms, Report Says,"
http://www.nytimes.com/2009/06/06/world/middleeast/06nuke.html

The Wall Street Journal, "Conflict is Inevitable Unless the West Moves Quickly to Stop a Nuclear Iran," August 31st, 2009.

UN, "NPT Treaty," http://www.un.org/events/npt2005/npttreaty.html

UN Security Council, "Security Council Toughens Sanctions Against Iran," http://www.un.org/News/Press/docs/2007/sc8980.doc.htm

UN, "Treaty on the Non-proliferation of Nuclear Weapons,"
http://www.un.org/Depts/dda/WMD/treaty/

US State Department, "Non-Proliferation Treaty,"
http://www.state.gov/www/global/arms/treaties/npt1.html

VOAnews, "Iranian-Run Bushehr Plant has IAEA Oversight,"
http://www.voanews.com/english/archive/2009-06/2009-06-10-voa60.cfm?CFID=261324429&CFTOKEN=16954979&jsessionid=88309314949620ce2a151e29325137861272

Washington Post, "Iran Is Critical as US Unveils Arms Sales in the Middle East,"
http://www.washingtonpost.com/wp-dyn/content/article/2007/07/30/AR2007073000623.html

Washington Post, "Iran Seizes 15 Seamen,"
http://www.washingtonpost.com/wp-dyn/content/article/2007/03/23/AR2007032300574.html